Advance Praise for

M000034974

Dan Newby and Lucy Núñez are the preeminent thought leaders in the domain of emotions. Their knowledge of and appreciation for the impact and value of emotions to shape our lives is conveyed in easy-to-understand ways in this book. As a coach, I use the distinctions they provide regularly to help clients expand their emotional range and develop new practices that lead to a more satisfying life. *The Unopened Gift* is an inspiring and indispensable guide for anyone seeking to more intentionally capture the power that lives in the emotional realm.

—*Kim Ebinger, Ontological Coach, U.S.*

Dan Newby and Lucy Núñez have written one of the most useful books on emotions that I have ever read. The authors take us on a journey of interpretation (not claiming to know the truth about emotions, which alone is refreshing) of emotions, from the theoretical to the practical. They present a cogent interpretation for what emotions are, but more importantly for me, how to understand emotions, work with emotions, and learn from emotions. This book contains the most comprehensive catalogue of emotions and how we can understand them better that I have ever come across. A most valuable resource for helping professionals, business leaders, and family members who want to be more connected to themselves and to those that they lead and care about.

—*Curtis Watkins, Master Certified Coach, U.S.*

Our work on emotions has been instrumental in fostering a culture of trust and stability in our school district. It is because of this learning that we have become a resilient, compassionate organization characterized by understanding each other first, then celebrating our growth and results

—*Julie Everly, Superintendent, Monroe Public Schools, Michigan.*

With this book, Dan and Lucy masterfully unveil our blindness around emotions. The book provides a powerful, actionable reconstruction of what emotions mean and how to distinguish between different emotions. I have seen no other book on emotions like this one. It clarifies the source of our emotions and invites us to take responsibility for our emotions, and hence our results. It is a must-read for leaders and managers who are emotionally illiterate.

—*Sameer Dua, Founder and Director, Institute for Generative Leadership, India*

This book takes to the next level what Daniel Goleman started with EQ. The thirst for working with emotions is increasing everywhere we look. A must-read for leaders, coaches, and anybody who wants to tap into emotions as fuel for action. Dan's passion of bringing ontological work into the world with his loving care for people and organizations is outstanding. I am grateful to have met him as a teacher, friend, and business partner.

—*Mirko Kobiéla, Senior Director Talent Management at Adidas Group and Founder of Luminize: International Coaching and Consulting, Germany*

This wonderful book is truly a transformational gift to anyone wanting to learn about the much overlooked domain of emotions and how they impact every aspect of our lives. The teaching in *The Unopened Gift* is practical and delivers the perspective of a true practitioner and not an academician. The compendium of distinctions on moods and emotions makes it an excellent resource for novices and a great reference for experienced practitioners. Finally, the potency of this material is just the tip of the iceberg of the transformational experience of working directly with Dan and Lucy.

—*Christian Stambouli, Projects Advisory and Team Performance Consultant, U.S.*

As a professional, husband, and member of society, this book has put an end to my long search for a practical and experiential path to emotional literacy. Really learning emotions vs. just learning *about* them is what you can get by immersing in reading this book. Dan and Lucy open a door to learning how to navigate emotions—which helps us human beings engage in life in many new and impactful ways.

—*Rafael García Monroy, Executive Coach and Trainer, Mexico and Spain*

Emotions drive behaviors which determine results. That's why emotional literacy is absolutely critical for human learning and development. *The Unopened Gift* makes a broad spectrum of emotions easily available to readers who would like to take a first step toward emotional literacy.

—*Reiner Lomb, Ontological Coach and Author of* The Boomerang Approach: Return to Purpose, Ignite Your Passion, *U.S.*

I used to feel guilty about myself because emotions I considered "bad," such as anxiety and fear, showed up very often in my life. *The Unopened Gift* opened up the possibilities of befriending my emotions. I feel liberated now, because it taught me that having those so-called "bad" emotions is not a limitation.

—*Jinobi Narain, Director, Learning and Development, Exucate Limited, Hong Kong*

Like many of us, I often struggled to manage multiple commitments as a business owner, mother, and "over-volunteerer." The emotional learning contained in this book has allowed me to put down my "Superwoman" cape and rediscover the power that I have to manage my commitments. It has definitely brought more peace into my life.

—*Jill Meaux, Coach and Consultant, Excelerant, U.S.*

THE UNOPENED GIFT

A Primer in Emotional Literacy

Dan Newby and Lucy Núñez

If you register at www.dannewby.me, ongoing updates and offers will be available. You will also receive access to a 30-minute video introducing Ontological Thinking and its role in leadership and coaching and its connection to emotions.

DEDICATION

This book is dedicated to our parents, Jesús, Rosa, Don, and May, who were, without doubt, the most influential teachers in our lives, and to our children, Suhail, Rachel, André, Will, and Octavio, whom we love deeply.

The Guest House

This being human is a guest house.
Every morning a new arrival.

A joy, a depression, a meanness,
some momentary awareness comes
as an unexpected visitor.

Welcome and entertain them all!
Even if they're a crowd of sorrows,
who violently sweep your house
empty of its furniture,
still, treat each guest honorably.
He may be clearing you out
for some new delight.

The dark thought, the shame, the malice,
meet them at the door laughing,
and invite them in.

Be grateful for whoever comes,
because each has been sent
as a guide from beyond.

Rumi
Translated by Coleman Barks

TABLE OF CONTENTS

PREFACE

Most of us believe that we're fixed emotionally, that the only way we can change in the emotional domain is through years of therapy or drugs. I used to believe that as well, but I don't anymore. For me, the big moment of revelation came during a time when I struggled with anxiety. I lived some dark, confusing, destructive years. My journey out of that time happened because of two things. One was that I engaged in a support group and learned what that had to teach me. The other was learning about emotions. I became emotionally literate. I came to realize that although I was fairly well educated in a traditional sense, I was emotionally ignorant. This was a part of myself that I didn't know anything about or understand even in basic ways.

Opening the door to learning about emotions required me to see my ignorance and relate it to the choices I made each day. I had to learn that the chaos I was living stemmed from my own emotional illiteracy and could only be resolved through learning. We humans are not as rational as we think we are. We reason and use logic, but we're not "rational beings." If we are rational beings, why do we have emotions at all? They would be unnecessary. But what if they exist for a reason? When we explore this idea, we become aware that we have overlooked one of the most important tools we have as human beings.

Do you have a partner or spouse? If so, was the selection of that person a rational choice? You may laugh, because choosing a partner or spouse is

1

often the least rational choice we could have made. After thinking this over for a bit, we all can acknowledge that what was driving that choice was emotions. Even if our parents had all kinds of reasons not to or our friends argued against it, we still married that person. The arguments, the logic, didn't matter. It's also true with buying a car, choosing a dog, or deciding what restaurant to eat at. It's true with everything. Is it rational to have children? Well, no, not really. It's not actually a great idea sometimes. But we do it. So then the question is, why do we do it? If we're just rational beings, we should be "smart" enough not to do those things that don't make sense, but we do them. So what's going on? What's going on is emotions, because emotions drive our behavior. And that's not good or bad; it just is.

MY STORY

In the days before I began learning about emotions, *fear* was one of the driving forces in my life. I experienced a great deal of *anxiety*. I didn't know the difference then, but they were both constant companions. There were other emotions too. *Loneliness* was clearly one, and a *lack of self-confidence* was another. But *fear* was the biggest. *Fear* of being alone, *fear* of being rejected, *fear* of getting in trouble, *fear* of getting caught, *fear* of losing my relationships, *fear* of everything. I would say that at that time I lumped all these emotions together into *anxiety*. Later, as I was able to name distinct emotions, I began to realize they were specific *fears*. But at first it was just this big ball of *anxiety*; I was *anxious* about everything. I don't know if what I experienced was technically panic attacks, but I suffered a lot. And I did what a lot of people do, which was to avoid the feeling. I did anything that might help me avoid the pain of fear. I worked too much, I drank too much, I watched too much television, and I even avoided my emotions by reading obsessively. These are all things I did because I enjoyed them, but during that time I was doing them to avoid emotions I didn't want to feel or acknowledge. In relationships I had a tremendous amount of *fear* that my partner would leave me, abandon me, and I'd be alone, so I tried to control the relationship. I tried to control the person. I was manipulative as a way to get things my way. But the main thing was to ensure that she didn't leave me—even if she didn't have any intention of leaving, which she didn't. In my mind, her every email, phone call, conversation or interaction was a potential threat. All the time I was thinking that "this is the thing that's going to cause her to leave me." It was a dark and confusing time.

From the support group I got the idea that what I was doing was running away from emotions. When I felt *anxiety*, I would try to get away from it through compulsive diversions like watching television or drinking. Whatever I did was for the purpose of avoiding my emotions. My mentors told me I needed to find a way to "be with my emotions." I had no idea what that meant. One day, not knowing what else to do, I decided that if I just sat still, I wouldn't have a choice; I wouldn't be able to avoid them. I had to force myself to literally sit on my hands so that I would remain still and experience the emotions I had been avoiding. It was strange and uncomfortable, but better than the pain and fear. I now realize that in that moment I quit running. I began to do this whenever I felt emotions overwhelming me. Sometimes it would be for five minutes and sometimes twenty minutes, although I can recall times when it was closer to an hour.

My real fear before I began to build an understanding of emotions is that they would kill me, literally, because they were so strong, painful, and scary. It sounds silly now, but at that time I believed it. Little by little I realized that, as bad as they felt, they were not going to harm me. I slowly realized I could learn that I didn't need to *deny* and avoid my emotions even if they were very unpleasant. Facing them and understanding them was going to help me even if I wasn't sure how. I got the idea that if I learned something about my emotions, they wouldn't be able to control me in the same way.

For me, desperation occurred when I hit such a low point that the only two choices were to die or do something different. The "doing something different" started with me attending the support group and going through a coaching course that taught me my first emotional distinctions. I began to realize how illiterate I was in the domain of emotions, and that, if emotions drive all our behavior, then surely I was behaving in the ways I did because of emotions. What was missing was that I didn't know which ones were driving me—that's what I needed to learn.

I had the great fortune of always being a learner. My parents were learners, and I was taught that learning is never wasted. So when I could see what I needed to learn or the area in which I needed to learn, things got much easier and I believed that maybe there was something valuable there for me. In the end, that made learning about emotions very logical, useful, and practical for me.

I first became aware of my emotions the day I sat on my hands without doing anything except observing my feelings. At first it was awkward, and I'm quite sure my first steps were inelegant. But little by little I learned to name them and realized that emotions sometimes feel similar, but are distinct. I began to understand that each emotion has its own story, and that if I listen to the story, even if I'm not sure what emotion I'm in, it tells me. I began to recognize distinctions, understand what emotions I was experiencing, how they were urging me to behave, and to question whether the subsequent behavior was something that was helpful in creating the life I wanted. I came to realize that learning about emotions was as important as everything I had learned intellectually up to that point in my life.

It would be giving me too much credit to say I realized any of that at the beginning. It was similar to beginning a journey by seeing a place that looks interesting and thinking, "Oh, there might be something there for me," and walking there. And when you get there, you see the next thing, and then you see the next thing. And then, at some point you realize, "Wow, I never had the intention of going on a journey, but that's what happened." And it happened because there was something useful continuing to move in that direction. For me, there was something that helped ease the pain and confusion.

That was really the beginning of my getting on the road, taking the first steps, and then having people support me when I wasn't staying on that journey. But also, there's something valuable about connecting with the pain of how awful it was to live in *anxiety* and *fear* and realizing that I was creating a lot of it through my own actions. It wasn't that somebody else was doing it to me.

Before, I always looked *calm* on the outside, but I never felt *calm* on the inside. I was always *terrified, anxious, doubting* myself, and *fearful*. On the outside I had learned to cultivate the appearance of *calm*, but inside I was not. Now I look *calm* to others and I feel *calm*. There are very few times when I feel *anxious*; it is rare that things *scare* me. There are not many times when I get caught by emotions. I experience emotions, but because I listen to them differently, they're giving me information. So when I hear myself thinking, "That's not fair," I think, "Wow, I feel resentful. What's that about? And is it based on anything real or is it just some story I made up?"

In the past, my emotions ran me. My emotions dictated what and how I would live my life. Now I would say I've befriended my emotions. They serve me. They don't control me. Of course, there are things I react to, but I have much more choice about how I'm going to respond out of these emotions once I've listened to them. So there's a lovely mix of reactions and responses. That was missing before. I didn't have any ability to respond; it was all reactive. The conversation in my head now is focused on embracing the emotion, accepting it, and looking for its value. Embracing an emotion also means not dismissing it as a complete invention. If I feel *fear* that my partner might leave me, then it might be a possibility, but fighting it isn't going to be beneficial. Trying to control her is not going to benefit anything. What's going to be helpful is to say, "I noticed I'm feeling *jealous*, not for any reason. I just have this *fear* that I'm going to lose you or that you're going to go away. I just want you to know that." In the past I would hide it because it was something I couldn't share; I couldn't talk about it because I was *ashamed* to admit it. If I had said, "I'm afraid you'll leave me," I thought that would push her to leave me. So there was even *fear* about *fear* in the past.

Now I would say there's *curiosity* about the *fear*. Sometimes I'm *amused* by the *fear*. I think to myself, "Come on, Dan. You're 61 years old, and you've been through a lot in life. You know how this stuff works. Don't get caught in this. Maybe she <u>is</u> going to leave you. Well, then you'll buy a motorcycle and tour Europe. You'll find something to do. You'll go work on an archaeological dig and you'll be happy, just in a different way." I've come to understand that neither story is true, but they produce different emotions, and I get to choose the story and the emotion I want to live in. The final realization that helped me to *accept fear* was that regardless of how close I am to another person, I was alone already. And it has always been that way. It wasn't that "One day I'll be alone." I will die alone, and whether I go first or second, that is how it will be. *Accepting* that reality was the final step because it allowed me to let go of trying to hold on to my partner. That step brought an enormous *peace* and ease.

Now I have completely different conversations with myself. To put it in my terms, I have different emotions about those emotions, but I would also say they're much less powerful, because when I feel *fear*, I can name it; when I feel *jealousy*, I can name it, and I know what it's trying to tell me. The emotion of *jealousy* is not trying to tell me to be afraid; it's asking me, "Are you really paying attention to this relationship? Are you doing everything you need to or you want to in this relationship? Or are you ignoring some things that you think would be good to pay attention to?" It's a pretty good question, because often I'm not paying attention to something that has an impact on the relationship. "So pay attention!" is what my jealousy says.

WHY EMOTIONS?

There are two emotions that allow us to begin a journey into learning about emotions. One is *curiosity* and the other is *skepticism*. When we are *curious* we would say, "I never thought about emotions this way. Tell me more, give me an example, show me how this works." When we are *skeptical* we say, "Wait a minute. That's not what I learned, so I'm not sure if I believe that." That is what *skepticism* as an emotion is intended for. It's supposed to help us figure out what to believe. "Am I going to believe what I learned before or am I going to take this new idea and believe it?" For those of us who have been very steeped in rationalism, who are very logical and cerebral, *skepticism* is quite common. It doesn't mean we won't learn or be open at some level; we're just going to be quite careful at the start. We want to make sure we're not getting tricked somehow with this "emotions stuff." And other people are *curious*. In the end they might believe it and embrace it or they might not, but they know they want to know more.

Emotions and moods are part of everything human-related. Each of us is continually experiencing emotions moving through us in response to the events within and around us. Whenever we are in the presence of other people, our emotions are being shared with and communicated to them energetically. Organizations are full of emotional energy that we are continuously trying to align. Leadership can be thought of as "the ability to generate the emotions required for the task at hand." If it is the case, as this book proposes, that emotions are "that energy that moves us into action," then the very existence of the organization depends on emotions. Although we often think of politics in terms of a lot of useless talk and the attempt to gain power, we will find the fundamental driving force of emotions underneath those actions. Marketing can be seen as a singular attempt to generate emotions that will provoke someone to buy a product. Successful marketing connects to and leads us into consumerism by leveraging particular emotions. Sports, although generally viewed as an activity of the body, would not exist without the emotions of *ambition, pride,* and *disappointment.* The arts, whether fine or expressive, are motivated by yet another set of moods and emotions. Eras in history are often defined by the mood of the time, and geography is often a strong generator of emotions and moods. Lastly, relationships between human beings—whether paternal, familial, or romantic—are all the result of and the origin of innumerable emotions.

It is safe to say that without emotions, humans would not exist. There would be no "reason" to have relationships, take care of each other, work, play, or create. We would not have "the sense" to avoid an oncoming train or not stand close to the edge of a cliff. We would not be driven to discover new places or to invent new tools. In fact, nothing human would occur. There would be no human activity. Of course, without emotions we wouldn't have ever become human; we would have perhaps stopped developing at the level of reptiles, and that would be the end of the story. Luckily for us, we didn't stop there.

Preface

Humans have long congratulated ourselves on our intellectual cleverness. We have used reason as a tool to meet the challenges of life, to build an understanding of the world around us that gives us a measure of control. And yet our ability to think and reason has not been sufficient to resolve the challenges we face and those we have created. But because reason is the one and only tool that we believe allows us to navigate life, the only possibility we have is to think and reason more. It is the very success of reason that has blinded us to other ways of learning and knowing.

There are two important reasons for me to pursue the work of emotional literacy. I believe that embracing emotional learning would change every human being's relationship with every other human being. It would allow us to realize and remember that we feel *disgust* not because the other person is *disgusting* but because that is the way <u>we</u> see them. The *disgust* isn't about them; it's about me. It's mine. It's my responsibility. The same is true of *anger*, *jealousy*, or *love*. When I experience emotions, they are my responsibility to be aware of and to act out in my life. It fundamentally changes a person's relationship with emotions when they take responsibility for them—all of them. I can no longer say, "It's okay to hurt this person because he or she made me *angry*." That is no longer justifiable. It is <u>my</u> *anger*; they are just the target. I'm *angry* because I believe something is unjust. That is what the *anger* is trying to tell me. I can react and punish or I can respond by trying to eliminate the injustice, but whichever I choose, it is still my *anger* and my responsibility. We are blind to this out of ignorance. We talk about others "making us *angry*," but overlook that they could have done exactly the same thing to someone else and it wouldn't have triggered anger in them, or someone different could have done the same thing to us and it would not have provoked *anger*. Until we take responsibility for our emotions and learn about them, we can't choose the ones that will support us and serve

9

the moment. Emotional literacy gives us an extraordinary tool to create the life we desire.

Embracing emotional learning would also change every human being's relationship with the world and with nature. There's a tremendous desire to have peace in the world. There is a growing desire to live in harmony with the natural world and to stop destroying that which makes life possible. What's in the way? What is in the way is emotional illiteracy. We don't understand emotions in a way that allows us to build what we want to build. Until we embrace the domain of emotional learning, emotions will have us rather than us having emotions.

My vision is that you will use this book as a step into emotional literacy and use it in all areas of your life. My hope is that what you learn from the book will support and enhance your relationships with your partner, family, and friends, and that it will be useful in your life pursuits, whether in teaching, health care, legal services, engineering, or any other area. Emotional competence is part of living a rich human life.

My best-case scenario is that this book will play a role in normalizing emotions so that they become simply a part of who we are and are no longer considered weird or uncomfortable. I believe that if more of us become emotionally literate, it will improve the world in the same way that literacy has.

At minimum I hope that upon finishing the book, a reader may say, "Well, I didn't really understand it all, but there might be something there." If all this book does is open a possibility of viewing emotions differently, I will be satisfied. If a reader comes away with one distinction—for instance, the difference between *service* and *sacrifice*—I'll be delighted. Even the smallest piece learned is valuable and will change your relationship with your emotions.

INTRODUCTION

How to use this book

Every emotion we have written about is important, but some are more common than others. Some like *anger, compassion,* or *doubt* are encountered daily, while some—*rage,* for instance—we might experience only once in a lifetime. You might think of the common ones as the middle ranges on a piano keyboard and the rarer ones as the very high or very low notes. All are useful and have a part in a rich composition, but some are used more than others. Sometimes our emotions are like musical chords—three or four notes at a time. Just as with understanding the elements of a chord, it is useful to separate the individual notes to understand them clearly and then see how they sound when played together.

As you read through this book, our hope is that it will provide you with a new way of thinking about emotions, and even more importantly, with tools you can use daily to make more sense of life. We have organized the book into four sections. The first lays out our interpretation of emotions and moods. The second section takes a look at more than 100 of the most common emotions we encounter in our work and how Lucy and I have come to understand them. The third brings this interpretation into the wider world of daily life and experiences, and the fourth is an alphabetical dictionary of

250 or so emotions that lists each emotion's etymological root, meaning, and purpose. This last section is designed to be a reference tool that can be used whenever you are looking for the understanding of a specific emotion. The index provided will also allow you to easily reference what we have included on any given emotion, so that you can use this book as a resource tool.

In this book we focus primarily on our interpretation of emotions and explore many distinctions. We are aware that much more could be written about emotions and their relationship to the body or biology, and much more could be explored in the area of culture.

We also have not given much attention to the question of how to work with emotions: "How can I shift my emotions?" "What are useful ways of practicing emotions I want to cultivate?" "How can I learn the finer distinctions?" etc. This is an endless and very personal exploration and may be the subject of future books. It is also the work we do personally in our coaching and workshops, and we invite you to contact us if this is of interest.

Human self-understanding is continually evolving, particularly in this area. If you have insights or examples you would like to share, if you notice emotions missing from one of our lists, or if you have an interpretation you believe could expand this body of knowledge, we would be grateful if you wrote us. This is work we are continually immersed in, and as a result, it is constantly evolving and taking on greater nuance. We welcome your additions. We can be contacted by email at dan@dannewby.me or lucynunez. alg@gmail.com.

Finally, you might be curious to know where this interpretation of emotions comes from. It is not our creation, but has emerged from a way of understanding humans focused on the entire being, which has been labeled *ontological*. Briefly, the ontological understanding of human beings is that we are more than simply rational beings and that emotions and the body are also legitimate domains of learning and knowing. The ontological perspective is that for the past four centuries we have increasingly seen ourselves as mainly rational beings and have come to believe that learning is solely an intellectual function. Coaches and teachers who embrace the ontological model work with their clients in language (the tool of reason) and pay equal attention to emotions and the body (somatics) in order to help formulate complete and sustainable learning. The ontological model does not in any way deny or diminish rationality, but puts it into relationship with these two other essential parts of our being.

Chapter 1

HISTORY AND CONTEXT

*T*hanks so much for your email. It came in the midst of my confusion. I cried *when I read it but, this time, the crying was good—felt nourishing.*

The emotion of "dignity" feels very right. I was trying to get to "hope" because I thought that that would be the emotion that would serve me. I could not get to "hope." Dignity was right there.

So, I have been wearing "dignity" for a few hours today and have come up with this declaration: "I will not stand idly by as people spew their ill-will and hate. I will stand up for my own legitimacy as a human being and for others. From this moment on, I stand to protect, cherish, and nourish humanity—mine, yours, and everyone else's."

Since I connected with my dignity I have noticed that I am no longer afraid to declare that I am a Muslim. After 9/11, I kept it quiet and avoided the issue as much as possible. If I disclosed, I often qualified it with a "but I am not like the extremists." I no longer feel the need to hide that part of my identity. Yes, I am still a bit scared, but not petrified, ashamed, or apologetic.

This email recently arrived from a former student and coach. She is someone who uses emotions in her work with clients but, as you can read, has learned to apply their power to her own situation. For us this letter is not just about her individual learning and journey but about our collective human journey. Understanding and even befriending emotions is one of the most powerful things we can learn as human beings.

Where We Find Ourselves

The central belief driving the writing of this book can be summarized in six words: "We human beings are emotionally illiterate." That does not mean there is anything wrong with us, but only that we have not yet learned how to understand emotions in a very useful way. It is similar to an illiterate person's relationship to written words. He or she can see the writing and understand that the markings have some value and purpose, but cannot figure out how to make sense of them. Although a few people may be incapable of learning to read, illiteracy is most likely the result of not having had the chance to learn. We see a similar possibility with emotions. Humans have tried many strategies, theories, and models to help us understand emotions, but have not yet found one that unlocks their meaning and usefulness. However, there is an interpretation of emotions that we believe does just that.

It seems that for most of human history we have been thinking about and trying to decide how to understand emotions. We have considered them as originating from thinking or from the body. We have thought about them being a result of biological balances and imbalances. They have been classified as a part of philosophy, biology, sociology, and psychology, but the consensus of most theories is that they exist as an inseparable part of our human experience, that to some degree they are part of our intrinsic makeup and the result of our experiences. The place we have arrived at in this journey is an uneasy and even suspicious relationship with emotions. We tend to see them residing in and emanating from the heart. We believe they are not trustworthy and that they compete with or are in opposition to thinking and logic. We see them as the opposite of reason and generally believe they need to be "gotten out of the way" in order to "think clearly." We believe they are fixed or at least very difficult to change and that they can only be changed with professional help. Our principal way of interacting with our emotions is to control or manage them, or at least to try. Beyond that, we often fear their power and believe life would be better if we had fewer of them. To some degree we relate to our emotions as if they are an infection or an alien being that has moved in and is doing all it can to undermine our constructive lives. In short, most people are not big fans of emotions and have, at times, wished they would just go away and leave us in the predictable world of reason.

Given this perspective, it is not surprising that we have left learning about emotions to chance. When we survey the subjects that constitute a formal education, the list will be long on cognitive or linguistic topics and will include almost nothing in the emotional realm. In essence we *hope* our children will learn about emotions, but we don't seem to know how to help them in a methodical or formal manner. Our expectation is that by loving them and telling them which emotions are desirable and which are not, they will learn enough. Even when they survive the turmoil of adolescence, it does not ensure they are equipped with emotional competence. Once we are adults, we assume that our emotional makeup is fixed and will not change; hence there is not much value in learning more emotionally unless it is related to an imbalance of what we refer to as our mental health. And in that case we tend to look first to medication rather than learning.

It may be the case with emotions that they are too close to us to notice them. Or it may be that we are aware of them but believe we can get away

17

with ignoring them. We may be afraid of them, or it could be that we consider them to be a no longer useful relic of our past in the way we regard our appendixes. Regardless of the reason, the fact that we do not see them as an indispensable part of ourselves leads us to dismiss their value.

It has been a common belief for a long time that emotions and moods are fixed and that there is nothing we can do to change them. The logical outcome of this view is that the only way to relate to emotions is to control or manage them. Most people understand emotions as things that are wired into us, and thus they are seen as things that *control* us. In this case, "us" is synonymous with our intellect, which we have come to see as our only reliable guide in life. So our habitual way of relating to emotions is that we do not trust them and we believe they cannot be relied upon. Most humans are at least uncomfortable with their emotions and in many cases are scared of them.

The Emergence of Rationalism

At least since René Descartes' statement "I think, therefore I am" in 1637, we have increasingly exalted reason over emotion as the basis of knowing. Until the past few decades, we have generally believed that "to know" was synonymous with cognitive comprehension. Whatever we wanted "to know" had to meet the rules of logic or reason or the associated disciplines of mathematics, physics, and other "hard sciences." Any "knowing" outside of these was suspect or ridiculed. This belief put the realm of moods and emotions outside of serious consideration as a domain of knowing and learning. Our narrow focus on reason and rationalism resulted in our abandonment of emotions as a domain of learning and knowing unless it was within the limitations of the "soft sciences" of psychology, sociology, and the like. But even those were not taken seriously as "real science," and hence were not thought of as "real knowing."

We also have for the most part ignored emotions as potentially valuable tools. We have banned or considered them suspect for a long time in organizations. This distaste for emotions in organizations is also historical in nature. During the Industrial Revolution, the concept of a group of people working together shifted from organic to mechanistic as the principles of the machine were applied to human beings. The word *organization* reflects the idea of groups working together being organic in nature. The word *work* and *worker* derive from a mechanical measure of effort. In our workplaces emotions are still trivialized at times and are almost always underappreciated because they contradict the mechanical nature of *work*.

In short, we have confused having emotions with being irrational. They are not the same, and when we do not distinguish between the two, we lose the potential of both. It is interesting to note that although Descartes' belief became an almost unstoppable force in Western thought, there were those who had other perspectives from the beginning. One of these was Blaise Pascal, a younger contemporary of Descartes, who responded to Descartes' claim by writing that "the heart has its reasons of which reason knows nothing." All along there have been those who did not see reason as the only way of knowing or even thinking, but it has nonetheless become our common-sense way of understanding ourselves and therefore the world.

Hyper-rationalism and the Devaluation of Emotions

As we have progressed along the path of seeing ourselves as rational beings we have, until recently, become more and more narrow in our view. We have approached a kind of hyper-rationalism that completely excludes any form of knowing except reason. In other words, reason is considered the ultimate and only valid way of knowing anything.

This book is based on the concept that the validity of an idea depends on its usefulness. We are not attempting to prove one thing true and another false, but rather to share a perspective that has been found useful and even life-changing by a growing number of people.

It is a tremendous help to our self-understanding as humans to consider emotions a domain of learning equal in value to reason. It is not more or less powerful. It is not more or less reliable. When the two are combined, they can produce a synergy we have not previously experienced and allow us to live more vibrantly and with a greater sense of self-assurance. Humans have long ignored the emotional domain, and by doing so, we have set ourselves up to be emotionally ignorant. The good news is that ignorance can be reversed through learning, and we have that opportunity with regard to emotions. In short, emotions can become one of our key supports in life. We can befriend emotions and we can learn to develop a higher level of trust in them.

The belief, at least in Western culture for the past few centuries, has been that emotions are at least suspect and at best unreliable; they are not to be trusted in making choices, and we need to take the emotion out of the equation in order to make sound decisions. The name we give to this is objectivity, and it is an idea from nineteenth-century science. In that time, it was believed that the observer of an object did not influence or affect the state of the object and thus was separate from the thing being observed. As it turns out, we have learned through quantum theory that this is not the case. The observer has been shown to be a factor in determining the outcome of the experiment, and the old idea that it was possible to be objective has dissolved. We can now see that at the moment of decision the emotions of the person deciding cannot be removed. Emotions are a part of the decider and thus a part of the decision-making. It cannot be otherwise.

Given this development in human understanding of the universe (that we are a part of), it's time to consider how we might see emotions through an updated lens as well. Besides demonstrating that "being objective" is not the possibility we thought it was, we have also learned that each of us is a different and unique observer. Thus what we see when we look at the world will depend more on us than on what we are looking at. In the area of emotions, this means that although you and I may both use the word "anger," we each have our own interpretation for what anger is, what it looks like, and how it feels. Our interpretations are likely to be similar, but they are not very likely to be exact. In fact, there is no way of knowing if they are exact. Thus any emotion can be said to have an *interpretation* but not a *definition* that applies universally.

Emotions and Learning

In the area of emotions, there is something key to be aware of in terms of learning. Because of the mechanistic influence on our way of seeing the world, we tend to think of learning as *accumulating information.* When we approach emotional learning, there is a distinction between *learning emotions* and *learning about emotions.* **Learning about emotions** is "taking in and understanding the concepts, the idea and the logic," all the cognitive ways we can learn *about* a thing. For instance, the way we *learn about cooking* by watching cooking shows on television. **Learning emotions** comes through spending time with them, sensing their energy, and naming them, experimenting with them, and practicing them; in short, through experiencing them and embracing them as if we were in the kitchen engaged in cooking. In a sense, it is learning from the inside out.

Full comprehension comes through marrying the conceptual and the experiential. And *knowing about* emotions can help us *know* emotions. This book presents ideas, concepts, and models that if adopted will allow you to experience your relationship with emotions in a new way. However, without creating experiences that include the emotions themselves, you risk only *learning about* emotions. This is, of course, true for learning anything deeply and completely, but because of our tendency to believe we are rational beings, we often fall into the limiting belief that knowing *about* a thing is the full story. With emotions it definitely is not. From this writing you can gain a large amount of cognitive understanding, but you will need to commit time to emotional experiences and reflection in order to gain a broader understanding of this domain.

Is it like? Or is it love?

When I lead group intuitive painting workshops, I witness people often get trapped by the need to like their painting. If they don't like their painting, they feel as if they have failed—done something wrong. In Dan's conference on emotions I experienced him making beautiful distinctions as to what it means to "like" something in life. He described how attachment to liking often produces a closed view in the world and how the emotion of love is often the one we are seeking or needing. I was in awe of how Dan was able to take people through this incredibly powerful territory without a paintbrush in his hands.

—J.C.

From frustration to calm

My realization came during a class I was required to attend as part of my work. I remember it like it was yesterday. I now know I was in the emotion of anger. I was dealing with my mother's death three months before. My father was in deep depression; his emotions changed by the hour, and he was drinking like a fish. My wife was not happy with the amount of time I was spending with him. My supervisor was the most difficult person I had ever worked for. The pressure for me was at its max. The next thing I knew, I was told I had to go to a class so I could learn a better way to communicate with colleagues, and that it would help me in my personal life. For me, this just made no sense at all. I was already behind in my job, and now I had to take three days to go "play" with my emotions. I was exhausted and I was angry that I didn't have a choice about going to a class I didn't want to attend.

The first morning I tried to block out the facilitator's voice. After lunch we started to talk about what emotions were and how we could understand them in a useful way. It was in that moment that I really started listening. The following day we went deeper into specific emotions. Wow, did I learn why my emotions were always frustration and anger. I learned how the emotion I chose to communicate from with other people made all the difference, and that was the day my life changed forever. I learned so many ways to be a positive leader, and how the human mind and emotions work in a practical way. Now I always think about what emotion I'm in before I answer any questions or make a decision. One major change for me is that I don't suffer from panic attacks anymore. Somehow, knowing that emotions are normal and just trying to tell me what is happening to me has made life much calmer and less scary. I never could have imagined it.

—L.Z.

Chapter 2

A NEW INTERPRETATION

All human beings share certain fundamentals. Breathing is something all humans do. Taking food for nourishment is another. Sleep is a third. These are aspects of being human that to some degree we have the power to choose *how* or *when* to do, but we do not get to choose *if* we will do them. Beyond these, there are other core aspects of being human that we sometimes overlook. One of these is that all human beings have emotions. Emotions are not discretionary. That is to say, we do not get to choose whether or not we will have emotions. We **are** emotional beings just as we are also rational beings. Although we individually relate to and express emotions differently, depending on our character, culture, and experiences, that doesn't change the fact that we all have emotions.

Fundamental to understanding what we are suggesting is that all of your beliefs about what emotions are and how they work are interpretations. They may be interpretations supported by research and experimentation. You may have accumulated data to "prove" that the belief you are proposing is the one and only truth, but if you dig deep enough, you will see that your belief is a particular interpretation of emotions. What we, the authors, are offering is simply another interpretation of the phenomenon of emotions. We are not claiming it is true, but we are endorsing it as useful and practical. Our years of experience as coaches, teachers, facilitators, and consultants have shown us that lacking a useful interpretation of emotions hampers our ability to engage in life in many ways. It makes us less effective in most things we do. It's often a source of confusion, because when we believe that humans are only rational beings, any event that cannot be explained rationally cannot be explained. Therefore it is not understandable within the boundaries we have created with our habitual way of thinking.

If you go to the dictionary for a definition of what an emotion is, you will generally find two statements: "An emotion is a feeling" or "An emotion is an affective state of consciousness." While both may have validity, neither definition is particularly helpful for understanding what emotions are, what role they play in our lives, what it might mean when we experience them, or how to navigate them. The ontological interpretation of the emotional domain allows emotions and moods to be understood as useful tools in daily life.

In the ontological interpretation, an emotion is what the etymology of the word suggests: *e-motion.* It is "that that puts you in motion" or "that which moves you." We all can notice the energy that urges us to move faster, change position, or say something we consider important. That energy is the emotion. In this case, "action" and "motion" are distinct from "movement." An emotion such as laziness will make lying immobile on the sofa attractive, which is its particular "predisposition to action." Emotional energy could show up as a reaction to an experience, which would be an emotion, or it could be more long-lasting, in which case we might call it a mood.

Both moods and emotions have the following specific attributes:

Emotions (and moods) are nondiscretionary

We **are** emotional beings. By our nature, emotions are present and are part of our makeup. Every human experiences emotions and moods. We do, of course, display emotions differently depending on our culture, history, gender, and other factors, but emotions and moods are present in every human being from birth to death.

Emotions are not always fun, and some of them are downright painful. Most of us have, at times, imagined what life would be like without that pain. We may have even tried to be "less emotional" or "more objective" as ways to try managing the discomfort. We may have tried to blunt the pain with distractions or avoidance. Those may work temporarily, but they are not useful long-term strategies. As much as a Spock-like way of life may attract us at times, it does not align with how we are constituted as human beings. Each of us has as an integral part the energy we refer to as emotions, the energy that moves us. And it must be so. Simply put, without that energy, human life would not exist. There would be no driver for sheltering ourselves and feeding ourselves, and relationships would be impossible.

An alternate strategy can be found within the emotional domain itself. Attempts to avoid emotions are actually the predisposition of an emotion: *denial.* As long as we remain in *denial,* we will be locked into this dynamic of trying to minimize our experience of emotions. Another choice would be *acceptance.* From our experience, this is an emotion that is not well understood or highly valued in contemporary society. Our default understanding of *acceptance* is that it means to agree, like, or endorse a thing. A more useful interpretation is that "I acknowledge it is as it is." In other words, we're not fighting against what appears to be a fact. We are no longer resisting, even though we might not always like or agree with events. We are simply acknowledging that emotions are a part of our human makeup, whether we like it or not, whether we agree with it or not, and whether we want it or not. When we apply acceptance to the idea that we are emotional beings, we are taking a step toward understanding them in a different way, which allows them to become a useful tool.

Emotions (and moods) are a legitimate domain of learning and knowing

Whereas previously we have believed that learning was primarily intellectual (using language as the carrier of information) the ontological interpretation is that emotions and moods are equal to intellect as domains of learning, knowing, and wisdom.

Think back on all your formal education. What pattern do you see about the criteria that made something worth studying? The one that stands out to the authors is that perhaps 90 percent of all our courses focused on cognitive or intellectual development. We studied information, knowledge, and (hopefully) how to think. Almost nothing of what we studied was even remotely focused on explicit development of emotions or the understanding of emotions. In our system we leave this learning to the social interactions that occur when we bring together large numbers of students, and it is primarily based on *hope*. We *hope* that our children will learn about their own emotions and the emotions of others, but we do not have a system that teaches them these things.

There are those who see the need and value of this, but societally we do not see moods and emotions as domains of learning. We grudgingly acknowledge them, but we mainly believe that they are "in the way" of learning. All readers of this book have grown up in a mindset we might call Cartesian. That is, we grew up thinking about the world based on ideas similar to those espoused by René Descartes, the power of reason among them. Growing up in any system of thinking makes seeing that system akin to a fish seeing water. It just looks like that is the way the world is. It looks like *The Truth,* and it is challenging to consider that it is just one of many ways of understanding the world. I remember a conversation with my son (born in 1989) in which I shared the experience of the world before personal computers. I would say that the emotion this produced in him was *incredulity*. At some level he could not imagine the possibility or what life was like when this tool did not exist. We can think of many examples of ways human thinking has changed over time. For us the idea that learning occurs mostly or only intellectually has the appearance of truth, but what humans are learning is that it is *not the best way* of understanding learning but *only the latest way* of understanding it. Just as the technology we use to interact with the world is changing and developing, so it is with what we might term *human technology.* The recognition of emotions as a domain of learning has vast implications in terms of how we see ourselves as human beings and the possible future paths open to us.

A common belief among our students and coachees is that emotions and moods are fixed. Often people express this by saying something like, "That type of situation always makes me angry; that's just the way I am," which reveals the underlying belief that there is no possibility of change or learning. Simply believing that emotional learning and choice is possible opens tremendous opportunities for human growth.

Emotions (and moods) are learned through immersion

They are different from intellectual learning, which happens through insight. Emotional learning occurs through immersion in the emotional energy, whether by spending time with our own emotions or by being immersed in the energy of others' emotions.

Having focused so much attention on cognitive learning, we are accustomed to the way it works. Intellectually we learn through insight. We see a situation, a pattern, a word, a mathematical expression, and something clicks. We see, in a flash, the logic of it. We gain or form an understanding almost instantaneously. You might say that the ease and speed of intellectual learning has spoiled us for other types of learning. Although *learning about* emotions can happen through insight, it will remain in the arena of the intellect. In order to *learn* emotions, we need to be immersed in them and experience them. It is learning of a different sort.

There are two primary ways of being immersed in emotions. One is by being surrounded by them, as we were in our youth with our family. Growing up, we absorbed our fundamental mood in this way. If we grew up surrounded by *fear,* we probably learned to see the world as dangerous. If we grew up immersed in the mood of *adventure,* we probably learned to see the world as full of interesting possibilities. Living with those who are trusting will have us learning the emotion of *trust,* and watching those around us giving freely will allow us to learn *generosity.* What occurs is more than just learning the habits of these emotions or hearing the stories associated with them; we also learn deeply in our bodies. Those moods and emotions we grow up with, we learn by default. But later in life we can choose which we would like to deepen and which we would like to diminish as drivers, and in that way engage in emotional learning.

The second way in which we experience immersion is by *being with* emotions, or perhaps more precisely allowing emotions to *be with* us. *Sadness* is an emotion that is not valued in the West. We tend to associate it with depression, and it goes against the grain of *ambition* and *enthusiasm*, which we favor more. We regard it as a negative emotion and don't believe that there is value in experiencing it. So when we feel sadness or others see us being sad, the usual reaction is to "get over it." Our friends or family will try to distract us or make us laugh, or we may choose to divert ourselves. However, when we feel an emotion, more is happening than just the experience of it. At the same time we are experiencing it, we are *learning it*. This may seem a strange concept, but imagine if it did not happen. Whatever level of *love* you were capable of and had for your child at birth would remain the same. It could not grow, which most parents find it does. If you did not grow up with generosity, you would not be able to increase it later in life; but in fact you can. The same would be true of trust or anger or wonder. We would remain static emotionally. So allowing ourselves to remain in an emotion until it has "finished its work" or "taught us its wisdom" is a primary way of learning through immersion.

Emotional learning has its own pace

While cognitive learning happens almost instantaneously, learning in the emotional domain happens over a much longer period of time. It isn't unusual for it to take weeks or months for emotional learning to take root.

Just as emotional learning has its own process, it has its own pace. As we said, intellectual apprehension happens very rapidly. When we are stumped or confused by a situation, we cannot predict when the insight will come. In the same way we cannot predict how long it will take for emotional learning to occur. We know from experience, however, that it takes longer than insight. If you consider that your mood in life was learned over the first 16 or 18 years of your life through family and cultural immersion, you can imagine that it might take some months or years to shift that mood. You might say that we have been spoiled by the ease and rapidity of intellectual learning.

Actually, there are two ways we already speak about these types of learning. One is that we "figure it out." That is to say we try to arrange the parts of the idea in a sensible order. This is how we arrive at an understanding intellectually. The other is that we "come to an understanding." This more accurately describes what is happening in emotional learning. Somehow the understanding arrives, but we may not be sure exactly how or exactly when. It generally requires patience, but is worthwhile when understanding comes.

We are never not in an emotion

This is horrible grammar, but it emphasizes the fact that there is never a moment when emotions are not present. We may not be aware of them or be able to name which emotions are present, but they are there nonetheless.

If we understand emotions as the energy that puts us into action, we can see that they are always present, whether we are busy or inactive. From the first moment of waking until we drift off to sleep, we will be experiencing one or more emotions. It is interesting to reflect on whether we experience emotions during sleep. One argument in favor would be how often emotions figure into our dreams and nightmares. Regardless of whether they are present in sleep, they are sometimes what rouses us to wakefulness, which would suggest they are constantly active.

At times people may tell us that they don't think they have emotions, or certainly not all the time. One possible reason this appears to be true to them is that either they are not in the habit of noticing their emotion of the moment or they do not know how to name it. We can gain the ability to notice our emotions by first checking what bodily sensations we are experiencing. Those sensations or *feelings* are what alert us to the fact that there is an emotion present. Many of us are not keen observers of these sensations. Given that we have not found direct ways of teaching emotions, it is not surprising that we sometimes lack the language to articulate the emotion we are feeling. A good beginning practice to build our emotional vocabulary is simply to begin naming the emotion we believe we are experiencing or which seems to be present. It is not as important at first to be correct as it is to build clearer distinctions. For instance, the emotions of fear, anxiety, and doubt tend to have similar sensations. Beginning simply with saying, "I feel something that might be fear, anxiety, or doubt" starts the process. From there we might reflect on their different underlying stories to more clearly identify which is the predominant emotion.

Emotions can only be known by interpretation

One can never see emotions directly but can only know them by interpreting how the body senses or displays them, or by the language we use to describe them (which is also a somatic function). Given that, it means that linguistically we can give any particular emotion an interpretation but not an absolute definition. I cannot know whether what I refer to as love carries the same sensations for others as it does for me. We can get a sense of the *playing field* we are on, but emotions are not empirical.

We claim that emotions do not have strict definitions, but it is possible to agree on useful interpretations of them. There is no definitive guide to what is and isn't an emotion or even to the meaning of any specific emotion. When we talk about emotions we are translating between domains—language and emotion—and the process is similar to translating between two languages or dialects. Anyone who speaks more than one language knows that often the best you can do is to try replicating the meaning, but that there is often something "lost in translation," and many words have no equivalent in another language. This does not mean it isn't useful to do the translation, but only that we need to be aware of this limitation so that we adjust our listening for greatest understanding. *Schadenfreude* in German has no direct translation or definition in English, but means something close to "pleasure derived from the misfortune of others." Our aim with emotions is to agree on a shared interpretation.

Differences of interpretation occur even within a single language. For example, when you hear the word "house," you have an idea of what it is, but when you begin to explain it in detail, the house you envision will differ from the house I envision. They are both houses, but we see them and describe them differently. The more we try to define a house, the more differences we will find, but we can probably find an interpretation we can both accept. To build an interpretation, it's helpful to investigate the etymology of the emotion. There can be a nuance in the original meaning or construction that helps us understand the reason the emotion was named in the first place. Language is invented on an "as needed" basis, meaning that when we face a situation or experience and do not have a word for it, we invent one. Generally, we invent one based on our observation of the human activity or our belief about where that activity comes from. Such is the case with the names humans have given to most emotions. This etymological search can be very rich and can greatly expand the depth of our emotional understanding. (In our work and this book the website www.etymonline.com was used extensively, and we recommend it as a resource.)

The most important element in getting to know your emotions is to focus on your own understanding and interpretation. If you can understand what the underlying story of *sadness* is for you, then *sadness* as an emotion will become useful even if the words you use to describe it are slightly different from the words other people use.

Each emotion or mood predisposes us to a specific action

In each distinct emotion or mood, our body *is inclined* to react in a specific manner. That doesn't necessarily mean we will act in this way, but that the emotions will make us want to act in a particular way. This includes what we may want to say, since speaking is a function of the body. For instance, joy predisposes us to celebrate; tenderness has us wanting to embrace; and anger, if it has its way, would have us punishing someone or something. We do not always act out the predisposition, but it is there, helps us identify the emotion, and will be modified by social convention and personal habit.

Anger predisposes us *to punish the source of the perceived* injustice. It is important to understand that it inclines us to do that, but does not force us to take the action. If we see someone kick a dog and do not see any reason for it, we may become *angry* and have the desire to hit or punish the person in some way. Social standards may keep us from taking that action, but the fact that we have the urge to punish tells us that we are experiencing the emotion of *anger*. *Joy* predisposes us to celebrate, *anxiety* to worry, and *ambition* to take advantage of the opportunities we see around us.

This is a place where we see a divergence between our ontological makeup and our cultural makeup. What we experience as predispositions tells us about the experience we are having as human beings, but that does not mean we need to act on them. Culture, including personal history, tells us what is appropriate behavior when we are experiencing that particular emotion. Being able to separate these is important in terms of understanding what we might call emotions in their raw state. That information then becomes a part of cultural interaction.

The following model illustrates various levels of identification we use. We each have individual attributes that we use as identifiers. Juan has dark brown hair, Linda has blue eyes, he is skilled with his hands, she is quick to understand, etc. We sometimes use the cultural level as an identifier by saying that someone comes from a certain country, has a particular ethnic background, or even does a certain type of work. The cultural identifiers identify what groups that person is a part of, whether they were by choice or not. The human or ontological level is the one this book is most concerned with. Every human sleeps, eats, and breathes. These functions are part of being human, and although we have some choice in when or how we do these things, we do not have a choice whether we will do them or not. Likewise, emotions are a part of being human. How we express them (or don't) and in what ways depends a lot on the individual and cultural levels, but having emotions is an aspect of the human/ontological level of our being.

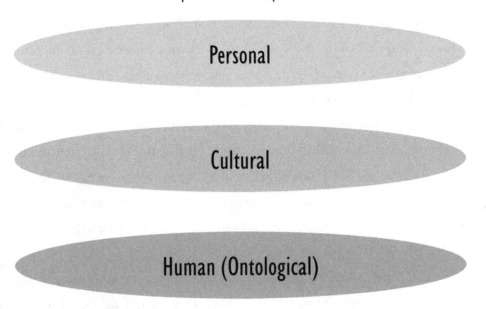

Every emotion is connected with a story or narrative in a co-creative way

In other words, emotions exist to provide information about our interactions with the world. When I feel ambition, I also am living the story that "there are possibilities for me in life, and I am going to go after them." When I am in the story that "It isn't fair" or "I shouldn't have to," the emotion of resentment is present. Again, these are interpretations and not strict definitions. The latter could be articulated differently and still be the energy of *resentment*. Emotions are not random or vague, but carry very specific information if we know how to decode them.

In the ontological interpretation, emotions and stories (or the thoughts) are co-creative. If you begin thinking about a time when someone *betrayed* your *trust,* you will notice it generates the emotion of anger and you may feel it rising in your body. Nothing that would provoke *anger* is happening at that particular moment except your thoughts about an incident that you believe was unjust. If we only considered this one sample, we might conclude that emotions are generated by thoughts. However, the reverse also occurs. Someone breaks his or her promise to you and it triggers *anger*. In the moment of identifying the *anger,* you may not have words to describe why you are experiencing that emotion. On reflection you may describe their actions as an injustice. In this case it appears the emotion generated the language you use to describe what happened. From a practical perspective, it is enough to show that there is a co-creative relationship between the emotion and the language. Experientially we probably can't tell which, if either, is leading, but we do know they are consistently aligned.

As it turns out, every emotion has just such a relationship with a very specific story. By "story" we don't mean your particular situation, but rather an underlying story that is consistent. Sometimes we call these beliefs our perspective or assessments. For instance, *sadness* is always connected with "losing something I care about." It is not simply about "losing something," because if you didn't care about it, you wouldn't feel sad. It isn't simply about "caring for something," because that also does not generate sadness. *Sadness* is always the story that you've "lost something you care about." Remember that we are interpreting from the domain of emotions into the domain of language, and you might word it a bit differently, but *sadness* always includes these two elements.

Frustration is the story that "I'm trying and it should have happened already." *Trust* is the story that "I am not taking an excessive risk if I interact with this person." *Fear* is the story that "something specific in the future may cause harm to me or someone I care about." We could continue with the several hundred emotions available to us as human beings. You can find the underlying story for many emotions in Chapter 10 of this book.

The value of being able to listen to the story of an emotion in this way can be remarkable. Simply from listening to a person speak, you can often come very close to knowing what emotion is provoking their conversation. That in turn allows you to ask questions that can help you both understand what they are experiencing. For example, if your son or daughter tells you they are "mad at you because you won't let them ride with a friend who just received her driver's license," you can instantly hear either *anger* or *resentment*. *Anger* would be their belief it is unjust and *resentment* would be that it is unfair. You also could know that your choice is based on a low assessment of *trust* (that allowing it is excessively risky in your assessment). Knowing these things allows you a more productive conversation than simply arguing or defending points of view. This knowledge allows a true conversation about care, responsibility, building *trust,* and how the two of you are different observers of the same situation. A work-related example might be that someone on your team seems disengaged in their work. Several emotions might fit that behavior. It could be *boredom* ("There is nothing of value here for me") or *preoccupation* ("It is more important to have my attention in another place") or even *resignation* ("Nothing I do will make a difference, so why try?"). The way to narrow down the field of emotional candidates is to listen to the person's story. If it is consistent with one of the three examples, you will know; if not, you need to look for the emotion that is consistent with their "story."

It is not essential that the story generating the emotion is true. If I believe someone has betrayed me, I will feel *anger* regardless of whether they actually have or not. If I believe I've lost something I care about, I will feel *sadness,* and if the thing suddenly appears, the *sadness* will disappear and I'll feel *happiness* or *joy.*

Emotions and moods often have a time orientation

Some emotions are concerned with or focus on the past, some on the present, and some on the future. In some cases the difference between two emotions is nothing more than this. *Regret* is the belief that life would be better if I had made a different choice in the past. *Uncertainty* is the story that I may make a choice that creates a future I don't like. *Peace, serenity,* and *happiness* are concerned with the present moment. Being aware of this time orientation can help us see if we are living in the present or are more drawn to the past or future.

Imagine a political candidate who talks about how well everything worked "in the good old days." Simply listening to the emotion underneath that statement tells you he or she is connected with *nostalgia* and that their efforts will probably try to take us back to a way of life that existed before. If the candidate talks about *hope,* he or she is looking toward the future and their energy will likely be put toward creating something new that they believe is better than the present (or past). And if that candidate said that things are fine as they are and we don't really need to change anything, you might hear *complacency.* Leaders of all kinds tend to focus on either the past or present because they are offering change. The main question is what kind of change. One is not necessarily better than the other, but the mood any of us live defines what is possible. *Resignation* is about the future and is based on past experience. *Resentment* comes from the belief that something in the past was unfair. *Awe* comes with experiences in the present, as do *wonder* and *curiosity.*

Emotions are not good or bad

Any particular emotion allows certain actions and interactions and not others. For instance, trust allows us to coordinate action with others. Lack of trust prevents us from coordinating action or makes it more difficult. Both have their place. A high level of trust allows us to build effective teams and to have dependable relationships. However, if someone does not have our best interest at heart and we perceive their insincerity, then it is prudent to not trust, and therefore not coordinate action with them. Resignation takes us out of engagement in life and may at times be exactly what we need to heal or rest. However, perpetual resignation (the mood of resignation) keeps us from interaction that we may deeply desire. By labeling emotions as good or bad, we cut off access to the ones we label bad. In essence we are throwing out their potential value and support.

This idea can be very challenging, because the current interpretation of emotions is so deeply entrenched. It is very easy for most of us to divide a list of emotions into the "good" ones and the "bad" ones. We tend to think of *love, commitment, happiness, peace,* and *enthusiasm* as "good" emotions and *sadness, rage, anger, frustration,* and *jealousy* as "bad" emotions. The unfortunate consequence of thinking about emotions in this way is that we strive to have more of the "good" ones and less of the "bad" ones. Sometimes this is taken to an even deeper level, and we attribute a moral quality to particular emotions. For instance, we may believe that *laziness* is not just a "bad" emotion but that it is "wrong." In this way we condemn anyone we consider *lazy* to be a bad or a lesser person. We do this with a whole range of emotions, among them *arrogance, anger, despair, greed, jealousy, envy, cynicism, resignation,* and *lust.* Likewise, we sometimes believe that people are morally superior when they often demonstrate good emotions like *ambition, enthusiasm, happiness, joy, hope,* and *love.*

41

Every emotion allows us to take certain actions and keeps us from taking others. If you consider *enthusiasm,* you can imagine its value in generating possibilities and exploring new ideas. In that sense, it can be of enormous value. But what if someone was <u>only</u> able to experience *enthusiasm*? What would they not be able to do? Resting, listening, or enjoying the moment probably wouldn't be available to them. *Anger* is an emotion many people are afraid of because it has been the source of hurt at some time in their lives. But what is the value of *anger*? It tells us what we believe is just and unjust, so if we did not have *anger* available, we would be ignorant about that part of ourselves. So the fundamental question about an emotion isn't whether it is good or bad, but whether it is serving us or not. Emotions exist to serve us and not the other way around.

Moods and emotions are not "chemically" pure

We often have several emotions or a combination of moods and emotions in a particular moment. These may be of a similar nature but also may seem paradoxical, such as when we have a *love-hate* relationship or we are *happy* for another's success but also *envious* of it. One does not contradict the other. Both are telling us something about how we see the relationship.

The idea of looking at emotions individually and separately is, in a sense, academic because that is not how they live within us. It is not unusual for us to experience more than one emotion at a time. For instance, we may feel *anxiety* and *doubt* in anticipation of an upcoming presentation. The *anxiety* has one message and function and the *doubt* has another. We may sense one more strongly than the other, but they both are playing a role in informing us about our experience. We may even experience what seem to be contradictory emotions, such as being *happy* that a friend is getting married and *envious* that they have something we don't but wish to. We may *like* someone but *distrust* him or her or even have a *love-hate* relationship. What if it was possible to honor all of our emotions, listen to their messages individually, and then consider how to respond? How different might life be? It is not necessary to deny emotions that seem to be illogical or paradoxical, and we may find that by listening to them, we gain important insights.

The same could be said for the relationship between moods and emotions. We might live in a mood of possibility or *ambition,* but might at times experience the emotion of *despair.* Again, they are telling us different things and inviting us to look at our whole relationship with the world, not just a part of it.

Every emotion takes care of a specific human concern

Emotions are often thought of as purposeless or as if they simply exist to make us uncomfortable. We disagree and believe that each emotion developed to take care of a specific human concern. Every emotion exists for a purpose. *Loyalty* takes care of the groups to which we belong. *Guilt* takes care of our private identity. *Anger* tells us what we believe is unjust and gives us the possibility of correcting it. We might say this is the *purpose* in having the emotion, and each emotion takes care of us in a distinct way. *Sadness* has the purpose of informing us what we care about in life. *Anger* tells us what we consider just and unjust. *Joy* signals that we see something in life worth celebrating. *Pride* says to me that I have done something I believe is good and that I want to tell others about it. The last chapter of this book proposes the purpose for each of the 250 emotions listed. Emotions then are not frivolous or random. They exist for a very concrete reason and have a remarkable role to play in taking care of us.

We are not our emotions

We experience our emotions, but they do not define us. Just as our thoughts are something we can consider and choose not to embrace or believe, our emotions offer us an understanding of the world around us, and thus they are a source of potential understanding. There is a distinction between "us having an emotion" and "an emotion having us."

One of the finer points of emotions and moods is that while they are something we continually experience, they are not "us." When we cannot distinguish between our core coherence and the energy of our emotions, we may confuse the two. Separating them is important because it allows us to stand back, notice, and reflect on our emotions rather than being caught in them. Understanding this difference allows us to choose between *reacting* and *responding*. *Reacting* is what we do when our predisposition happens more quickly than we can think. It has been shown that our emotional reaction time is shorter than our intellectual response time, and so this will happen "before we know it." However, it is also possible to train ourselves to make space between experiencing an event and reacting, or even to learn a different reaction to our native one. This is the work athletes are constantly immersed in to improve their physical performance.

It can be valuable to build the capacity to respond rather than just react, since reaction may not be the most effective way to resolve the situation you are facing. Imagine that you are angry because you believe someone has done something unjust to you. Perhaps you have not received a pay increase when all signs were that you would. *Anger* will predispose you to punish the source of the injustice, in this case perhaps your boss. So you might say something damaging to him or her, you might become sullen in your attitude, or you might begin saying negative things about your boss to co-workers. However, none of those actions will correct the injustice. The effective way to approach the perceived injustice is to seek understanding. "Is it true there will be no increase in my compensation? What is the context of that decision? Was there something in my performance that didn't warrant the increase?" On what were your expectations based? Was there a promise that was not fulfilled? Asking these questions would be part of a response and will set you up to make changes to take care of the injustice. Perhaps the solution will be to change jobs, change bosses, work harder, request honest feedback, or learn to avoid building expectations. All of these are probably more effective than simply punishing your boss, but can only be done with the practice of choosing your response rather than reacting.

Emotions are triggered; moods are not

The distinction we draw between moods and emotions ontologically is that emotions are triggered by an event, whereas moods are pervasive energies. What this means is that emotions are provoked by an experience, whereas moods shape the experience we are having. If one lives in the mood of fear, they will see the world filled with danger, and that will shape their behavior. If the mood is resentment, they will see the events that happen to them as unfair, because the mood is the lens through which they assess their experience. Put another way: Moods exist before the experience; emotions follow the experience.

Emotions are the reaction to an experience. They are triggered by something, whether it is a thought, an encounter, something you see, or something someone says to you. You generate a story from that trigger, and that story will elicit its related emotion. This interpretation does not support the idea that others "cause" us to feel certain emotions. So when we say "he made me angry," it is a poor representation of the process and actually puts us off course trying to understand what is happening within us. Part of becoming emotionally competent is taking responsibility for our emotions and realizing they are ours to understand and navigate. This can be challenging at first, because the habit of blaming others for how we feel is long-standing and is generally easier than taking the responsibility.

Moods are not triggered by an event but actually precede our experiences and shape our understanding and interpretation. When we are in a mood of *fear*, all that we see around us appears dangerous. If we are in the mood of *gratitude*, we see a world full of gifts. If *ambition* is our base mood, we will see a world full of opportunities, while in *resignation* we will not try to take action, as we believe nothing we can do will make a difference. Moods can be thought of as the lens through which we see the world, and they shape our interpretation of the experience. In this way they are distinct from emotions proper.

The existence of emotions is logical

It may seem paradoxical, but the existence of emotions is quite logical. If we understand the purpose of our cognitive skills to be the gathering and sorting of information, it is logical that we would need a mechanism to weigh the value of that information. This is the role emotions play in the ontological model.

Many of us grew up with the idea that reason and emotions were opposites or worked against one another. The belief has been that we cannot operate in both logic and emotion at the same time or that one contradicts or counteracts the other. In that interpretation, emotions are not logical or connected with reason, and vice versa. Recently significant research has demonstrated that our decisions, actual choices, are always the result of emotions, which is in line with the ontological interpretation of emotions as "the energy that moves us." Our intellect or neocortex is designed to accumulate and organize data, but it does not have the capacity to choose. Choices are made due to *desire, annoyance, care, frustration,* and a wide range of other emotions. The energy of the choice is always emotional. Since reason cannot choose, it is logical that humans need a mechanism to discern what is most important in order to act on it. That is the role of emotions. So it is logical that humans developed emotions and that they are indispensable in all aspects of life.

A parallel idea can be seen in the development of artificial intelligence. The logic algorithms have been fairly well worked out and continue to improve. The biggest challenge in this area of development is to find a way the artificial brain (neocortex) can discern the value of the possible choices (precursors to action) it has. This is precisely the role emotions play in humans.

Our emotions are the result of how we're made plus what we've learned

The eternal "nature vs. nurture" question is evident with emotions and moods. Certainly we are wired in a particular biological way as human to have the capacity for emotions and individually to the way we process them. And there is a growing body of work that demonstrates how we learn in the emotional domain and how emotions are a part of the learning process.

From our own study and experience, it is impossible for us to say that one is more important than the other or to deny one in favor of the other. It seems that a more useful question is "How much of who we are is constituted by the way we are made vs. what we have learned?" This seems to vary from individual to individual, as do many other human attributes. Each of us is "wired" in a particular way in terms of native structure. The rest is learned, and the two are continuously interacting, so the ratios change over time. One can always try to learn, and if even small changes occur, it shows that learning is a possibility. Even if there is not a change, one can continue trying to learn as long as there is persistence and hope. But if one does not try to learn, it is not possible to know one's capacity for learning in the emotional domain.

To enter into emotional learning, the first belief most people need to challenge is that "the way I am is fixed." People often express this, saying, "That is just the way I am." To open the possibility of learning, we suggest changing your conversation to "that is the way I've learned to be." In fact, no one can say to what degree you can learn emotionally, but we have found over the years that a great deal can be learned in this domain that we have always considered fixed.

Caring about someone vs. caring for them

The conversation I had with Dan that was very helpful to me occurred at a reception overlooking the mountains. He and I were enjoying our meal together, and he talked of his experience falling in love with his bride. Two things I remember. "Lead with the body," and ask simple questions. "Are you hungry? Are you cold?" At that moment I realized the deep importance of care as an emotion. Dan went on to share that sometimes we care about someone but they aren't aware of it because we don't care for them. That distinction has stayed with me, and I often ask myself whether I'm demonstrating my care in such a way that the other person understands its depth. It was a simple lesson, but has made a big difference to me.

—K.R.

Chapter 3

THE MEANING OF EMOTIONS

What Emotions Are Telling Us

Expertise in any field is based on the ability to distinguish and name critical elements. An attorney recognizes distinctions about the law and legal process while a chef recognizes distinctions about foods, flavors, textures, and cooking processes. In the domain of emotions, our ability to distinguish emotions by name, by their sensations in the body and by their story, is what gives us increased competence and expertise. Calling a particular activity *service* or *sacrifice* interchangeably means we are not clear on what they are and betrays the limits of our emotional knowledge. The more finely we can understand the nuances of distinct emotions, the more emotional intelligence and emotional competence we will have access to.

Given that articulating emotions in language is a form of translation, it is impossible to *define* emotions absolutely. We can, however, establish a meaning and find an interpretation that allows us to work with them closely. The most important thing to understand linguistically is the interpretation, as Ludwig Wittgenstein pointed out in his study of the philosophy of language a century ago. After fifty years of living in and traveling through many cultures, our personal and professional experience is that we have not encountered a culture that did not have an emotion that is triggered when one has the experience of injustice. That experience seems to be universal. In English the name of the emotion we assign to that response is *anger*. When translated into other languages it may vary, but it seems such an emotion exists in all cultures. Our own belief is that all emotions are available to each human being at some level. Perhaps due to variations in biology the availability or intensity of emotions differs among individuals, but the greatest variation in our relationship with emotions is what we have learned about them. Part of every culture's makeup is its relationship with emotions. Each culture has a unique understanding of what emotions are and values or pays attention to some emotions more than others, but here again we are taking a look at the human or ontological level of ourselves. Below are emotions we encounter most often in our work. This list emerged from our own experience, and thus is strongly influenced by Western culture. A list with a different cultural orientation—indigenous, for example—might differ. A longer list is available in the Resources section at the end of this book:

- **Acceptance:** *Acceptance* is one of the least understood and appreciated emotions, which is unfortunate given its possibilities. The default belief is that *acceptance* means "giving in" or "giving up." It is often confused with *resignation* and can be regarded as a sign of weakness. Ontologically, to *accept* means to "acknowledge it is so." It means that we are not resisting what has happened or is happening and that we are seeing life as it is. It **does not** mean that we agree, like, or endorse how things are. It only means we see things as they are.

  When we hear someone say "whatever," they might be expressing *acceptance* or they could be experiencing *resignation*. *Resignation* is the story that "nothing I do will make a difference, so why try?" The confusion comes because both emotions appear inactive. The predisposition of both is stillness, so we need to look closer at the slump of the shoulders (or not), the downcast eyes (or not), or the exhalation of breath that says, "I give up" in order to see the difference. The other route is to investigate what the person is thinking—their "story"—and this will point to one or the other more directly.

It is a common belief that *acceptance* is difficult to achieve and takes a long time. The expression "come to acceptance" reflects this thinking. However, it is possible for us to declare *acceptance*. When we feel exhausted by revisiting a past experience or irritated that we are stuck, we have the opportunity to decide that we are done with that emotion or thought. Linguistically this is done by making a declaration, which is a statement that, when made by someone with the authority, begins or ends something. The change will not be instantaneous, but the declaration puts us on a road to a new way of thinking and a new emotion. By consistently redeclaring our acceptance that "it is so" or "I'm finished thinking in that way," we can open a new direction. Over time this can generate acceptance or peace that allows us to move out of resistance. The aim isn't to remain forever in acceptance, but that it is a stepping-stone to another emotion such as ambition or enthusiasm, and it is one that cannot be skipped.

Imagine that you awaken in the middle of the night and do not fall asleep again immediately. Lying there, you may find yourself fighting against the fact that you are awake. You might think about how tired you were when you went to bed and that you can't believe you are awake. Or perhaps you begin to worry about the meeting you have in the morning and fear being tired when you have to present your part. You might begin to hear the noise of your partner breathing or the neighbor's dog barking. The pattern you enter into is resisting being awake. That is, you do not *accept* that you are awake in the middle of the night. If you were to decide to *accept* being awake, it would not mean that you like it or want it to be that way, but only that "it is so." Once you declare your acceptance, you may begin to see alternatives. You might think about reading a book, writing a letter to your mother, or simply appreciating the moonlight shining through the window. Those things were not available to you until you *accepted* being awake.

A great deal of time and energy is spent fighting against what is. Sometimes it is important for us to resist the way life is, but often we resist out of habit and reflex rather than because our wisdom directs us. Adding *acceptance* to our toolbox of emotions can be a significant move.

■ **Accountability:** "Willing to be called to account," "answerable for our actions," or "accepting the consequences of our decisions" are other ways we could think about *accountability*. Its purpose is to keep us "true to our word" or to keep our actions aligned with our commitments. This has the effect of generating coherence between our "being" and our "doing" and gives us a reliable identity. It should be noted that *accountability* alone does not make us a "good" person in any way. You could be *accountable* to the rules of a community that require you to kill disloyal members, and while you might be absolutely *accountable*, it would not mean that you are ethical or caring.

■ **Admiration:** Our word admiration comes from Latin *admiror*, "to wonder at." When we experience *admiration*, it means we would like to do things the way others do them. For example, when I started in the field of training I was a participant in a workshop and had a wonderful coach. My thought was, "When I'm a coach, I'd like to coach like him." Some people interpret *admiration* as putting the other person on a pedestal, but ontologically we would call that emotion *worship*. *Admiration* doesn't put the other person above me but rather tells me that something about the way they live or do what they do appeals to me, and I would like to emulate that way of being. *Admiration* is the emotion that tells us what we aspire to and motivates us to pursue it.

■ **Ambition:** Comes from the Latin word *ambitionem,* which means "a going around," especially to solicit votes. It is appropriate then that we often think of politicians as *ambitious.* In Western culture we tend to have a love-hate relationship with *ambition;* we see it as a good thing to a point, but also find it distasteful or annoying when it is someone's predominant mood. In certain cultures—the United States, for instance—*ambition* is thought of positively, whereas in others it is considered vulgar or associated with aggression.

■ **Amusement:** *Amusement* comes from French roots and has to do with diverting our attention or causing us to ponder something different. It is not necessarily something that makes us laugh, but is often something that makes us smile. The purpose of *amusement* as an emotion is to inform us that we are experiencing something unexpected and enjoyable. *Amusement* can be an antidote to *gravitas* or *seriousness*.

■ **Anger:** When *anger* arises, it signals that we are encountering a situation we believe is unjust. It does not mean the situation is unjust, but that is our interpretation. If we did not have that interpretation, we would not experience *anger*. Anger is one of the emotions that we are most afraid of, because the predisposition of *anger* is to punish the person we believe responsible. When we do this as a strong reaction, it can cause injury to the person or to the relationship. Sometimes for this reason we try to deny or hide our *anger* rather than find a way to channel or navigate it. Many people believe that the emotion of *anger* is synonymous with the drama sometimes used to express it, but that is not necessarily the case. *Anger* can be expressed very calmly, because the story of "perceived injustice" is actually the most important part. The value of learning to *respond* out of emotions rather than to *react* out of them becomes clear with *anger*. Simply punishing the source of injustice doesn't necessarily remove or eliminate the injustice. It may feed our sense of *righteousness* but not be the most effective way to deal with the situation. Reflection on what would be needed to eliminate the source of the injustice can lead to actions that truly create change.

Imagine a life without anger. Lack of anger would mean we would have no way of knowing when we believe something is unjust, and so would not know what we believe is just. We would not be able to defend ourselves from those things we believe unjust. We would do things because they were expedient or fun, not because we believed deeply they were the "right" things to do. It is unlikely we would have systems that aim to protect children or animals, human rights would not have anger as an emotional basis, and we truly would live in a world where "might makes right." That scenario is a terrifying prospect. Before we label *anger* one of the "bad" emotions, we might stop to consider how life would be without it.

■ **Anguish:** The name of this emotion comes directly from the somatic experience of it. *Anguish* comes from the Latin and means "to tighten" or "to throttle." When experiencing it, we can barely breathe. When a child dies or a person is displaced from their homeland, *anguish* might appear. The predisposition of *anguish* is to struggle for understanding, and it informs us that the world as we know it is collapsing. Anguish exists to help us move toward a changed life.

Annoyance: *Annoyance* is rooted in the Latin "to make loathsome" or "to make hateful." In other words, it tells me what I do not want to participate in or have as part of my life. It is an emotion that utilizes discomfort to get our attention and convey its message. At a low level we will tolerate a situation, hoping it will change, but when the *annoyance* surpasses our ability to ignore it, we will look for ways to change the situation. It is one of the many emotions that orient us to what we do and do not want as part of our life. Examples could be as varied as ill-fitting shoes, a fly that keeps circling our food, or noise from the street when we are trying to sleep. If the level of annoyance surpasses our tolerance, we will take some sort of remedial action.

Anticipation: As an emotion, *anticipation* is sometimes expressed by saying we are "anxious" for something to happen. This shows the degree to which the two terms feel similar. *Anticipation,* however, means to "take care of ahead of time" or to be involved with something before it happens, whereas *anxiety* is waiting for something unknown to happen. An example of *anticipation* would be when a manufacturing company has changed to more modern machines, has taken care of all the details for implementation, and is waiting to see what the results will be, assuming they will be positive. *Anxiety* would be the belief in this situation that "something will probably go wrong."

■ **Anxiety:** Our emotion "anxiety" comes from the Latin *anxius*, "solicitous, uneasy, troubled in mind," and from *angere, anguere*, "choke, squeeze," figuratively "torment, cause distress." Most of us can relate to the physical sensations we experience in *anxiety* from this description. When we experience *anxiety*, it is connected with the story that something now or in the future may harm us, but it isn't clear where the harm will come from. The "not knowing" can be a form of torment, distressing, and "a troubled mind" is a fair description of worry. In this it is different from *fear*, in which we can identify the source of the harm. The discomfort we experience in *anxiety* is designed to get our attention about a possible danger and to challenge us to look for a specific source. This happens through worry, which is the predisposition of *anxiety* and signals its presence. One way to navigate the worry and *anxiety* is to try to turn it into a *fear*. If we can name the source of the possible harm, then we can often take actions to diminish or eliminate it, but we first need to know what we need to change. Another possibility can be to elevate the emotions of *courage* and/or *boldness,* which allows us to move ahead in spite of the anxiety and, in essence, meet it head-on. *Anxiety* can be the result of a chemical or biological imbalance, in which case support would need to come from a medical or therapeutic source.

■ **Apathy:** *Apathy* is the story that "I simply don't care." It literally means I am "without feeling or emotions," but ironically is itself an emotion. In *apathy* our predisposition is to "not take action" or to leave the action-taking to others. Immobility and lack of engagement are ways in which it shows up. *Apathy* differs from *boredom* in that the latter can move us to look for activities where we find value rather than simply being immobile. Of all the other emotions, it is probably closest to *resignation,* where we believe nothing we do will make a difference. In *apathy* it isn't that we believe we cannot make a difference but that we do not care if we make a difference. Apathy is an emotion that can be commonly observed within organizations, since they are places where making decisions, generating results, and being proactive are highly valued. When someone is in the emotion of apathy, it is very evident to all, because we perceive a void of acting in alignment with the organization's goals.

Apologetic: *Apologies* are deeply misunderstood. Most of us learned that to *apologize* means to say, "I was wrong." Saying I'm wrong is actually driven by an emotion like *accountability* and is separate from being *apologetic*. To offer an *apology* means that "I am aware that something I did (or didn't do) may have harmed you." It is not an admission of wrongdoing. An *apology* is appropriate when *we* believe we have done some possible harm, even when the other person may not be aware of the incident. So *apologizing* is something we do to show we take responsibility for our actions and want others to know. The harm we believe we have done may or may not be apparent to the other person, but if we believe we have done something that might have caused injury, the appropriate step is an apology. If we separate "unintentionally causing harm" from "being wrong," we can more easily offer apologies. The sincerest apology is when we offer it because we believe we've caused harm. We can, of course, *apologize* when the other person requests it, but it is still not inherent in the *apology* that we did something wrong.

Appreciation: "To esteem or value highly," from Late Latin *appretiatus,* "to set a price to." The emotion of *appreciation* allows us to *enjoy* the value of a person or thing. It does not necessarily have a physical action associated with it, although we often resort to language to express the emotion. As with *admiration, sadness,* and other emotions, *appreciation* tells us what we value in life. Appreciation requires looking beyond ourselves in order to see others. It also requires the recognition of the value of others. For that to happen, we must know what value looks like within our context or relationship. The most important aspect of this emotion is that it lets others know we are aware of them, value them, and believe they are doing something of value. That in itself is a tremendous motivator for many people.

Arrogance: What is it about someone that makes us think of them as arrogant? A big clue comes from the Latin etymology: *Arrogantia*— "assuming, overbearing, insolent." If we look at the definitions of these three words—*insolent* being "a haughty disregard for others," *assuming* being "receive up into heaven," and *overbearing* meaning "the weight of physical force"—we get a visceral sense of the emotion. Those who are in the emotion or mood of *arrogance* think of themselves as above others, somehow on a heavenly level, and having the right to put weight on others. Their story is that they are superior to others and of greater importance. The disposition of *arrogance* is often seen in verbal condescension toward others, but can also be seen in the way people carry themselves. The expression "looking down your nose" aptly describes a physical disposition of *arrogance.* So what purpose does *arrogance* have for us as human beings? (Because if it didn't have a purpose, humans would not have invented it.) *Arrogance* is useful as an emotion, as it allows us to get things we don't otherwise have the power to obtain. If we behave as if we are superior, smarter, or more moral than the other person, it is a way of gaining the advantage as long as the other person believes it as well. In a sense, *arrogance* is similar to *righteousness* in action. Both are based in a story that "I know best," but arrogance has the added element that "this makes me a better person than others are."

■ **Awe:** The root of the word *awe* is Northern European and blends *terror* and *reverence*. The thing we are *in awe of* both *scares* us and commands our *respect*. This is an emotion often associated with encounters with the divine or with powerful natural events such as hurricanes, earthquakes, or erupting volcanoes. They attract us, sometimes tremendously, and at the same time terrify us. Clearly the slang expression *awesome* derives from the original meaning, but has lost its depth.

■ **Betrayal:** To feel *betrayed* comes from believing that someone has intentionally and secretly "handed you over to the enemies." When you discover the deception, it triggers the emotion. The purpose of the emotion is to help us distinguish those loyal to us from those disloyal to us. It is an indicator of who we can trust and who we cannot.

■ **Bliss:** *Bliss* derives from the Old English *blis*, also *bliðs:* "bliss, merriment, happiness, grace, favor." It is co-creative with the story that "all is right in life," and in *bliss* we feel light and relaxed. Joseph Campbell, a pioneer in the understanding of culture and emotions, chose *bliss* as the emotion that points to one's life purpose. *Bliss* has similarities to *serenity, peace,* and *acceptance*. All give us the opportunity to reflect, appreciate, and enjoy moments in life, but only *bliss* has this connection with life purpose.

■ **Boldness:** *Boldness* allows us to take the actions required to confront a situation which we fear or dread. The opening to the *Star Trek* television show and films uses it in just this way when the narrator says: *"Space: the*

59

final frontier. These are the voyages of the Starship Enterprise. Its five-year mission: to explore strange new worlds, to seek out new life and new civilizations, to boldly go where no man has gone before." One can be *courageous* but yet not take actions that *boldness* allows. While the word *courage* comes from Latin for "heart," the Old English equivalent is *boldness.* They are a bit different in that *courage* is "having the heart" or strength to face what we are afraid of, and *boldness* allows us to use that strength to take action.

■ **Boredom:** To be *bored* is a message that "there is nothing here for me to benefit from." It does not mean there is anything wrong with the book, lecture, or relationship with which I am *bored,* as we often think. In this sense, *boredom* is a highly useful emotion as a guide to those things in life that are interesting, engaging, and likely beneficial, and those that are not. We think of things, situations, or people as *boring,* but in fact the *boredom* is in us and is trying to tell us something about ourselves. We have a strong moral interpretation in which we think of someone who expresses *boredom* as a bad person and someone who is always engaged as a good person. If you aren't sure this is true, consider that we generally give students lower marks if we perceive them as *bored* or not engaged rather than teaching them the benefit of listening to *boredom* and pursuing something of greater interest. A useful way to listen to *boredom* is to turn it into a question. For instance, if I find myself *bored* with a book I am reading, a useful question is whether there is any use in me finishing it. If it is a movie, "Should I consider leaving midway to do something more beneficial to me?"

■ **Calm:** *Cauma* in Latin referred to the heat of the midday sun, when everything was still. That is very much what *calm* means to us today although, of course, it is an emotion that can show up at other times and in other situations. Its origin makes it easy to see that when we are in a moment of *calm,* the most natural thing to do is to rest. And given the co-creative nature of stories and emotions, one can choose this emotion when needing stillness and rest.

Care: The linguistic root of the emotion *care* in Old English meant to "be anxious, grieve; to feel concern or interest." In other words, we take an interest in someone or something, and what happens to it or them is important to us. This interest comes from a connection we have that might be familial, or a shared background or an experience that impressed us in the past. It is quite common to hear the story of someone who, for instance, became a pediatric doctor because he or she had a sibling who needed urgent medical attention when young. Whether the sibling got the medical attention or not, that experience had such an impact that the doctor chose children's medicine as a career. Other stories in the same vein exist for most vocations and avocations, such as the child who grew up in awe of the forest and became a forester or an environmentalist.

A useful distinction regarding the emotion of *care* is that we can "care about" things and people or we can "care for" them. The difference is that *caring about* something or someone does not require time and energy. *Caring for* someone or something does. We can care *about* an almost unlimited number of things or people, but since humans have limited time and energy, we can only care *for* or *take care of* a small number of things. Many people believe that if they are not *caring for* a thing or person, it means they *don't care. Caring about* something can be seen to have its own value apart from *caring for* it.

■ **Caution:** To be *cautious* means to "be on one's guard," which implies we believe there is possible danger in a situation. Caution is usually connected with a previous unpleasant experience. The idea is that we need to take small steps and build trust before we take the next step, in order to remain safe, because in the past it has not been safe. *Caution* and *prudence* are quite similar in their actions, the difference being that *caution* tends to be related to action while *prudence* is more concerned with making choices. The purpose of both is to keep us safe by taking possible danger into consideration.

■ **Celebration:** From Latin *celebrare*, "assemble to honor," also "to publish; sing praises of; practice often." In the emotion of *celebration*, we are inclined to gather a group together to praise something or someone. We could *celebrate* an athlete, the harvest, or a new invention. We *celebrate* birthdays, anniversaries, and weddings. We don't typically *celebrate* something like a divorce because we do not consider it honorable. If we did, we would celebrate it. When we hold a funeral, we are not *celebrating* death but are coming together to honor the person who has passed.

■ **Commitment:** *Commitment* is the emotion that has us acting in concert with our promises by putting our whole being—body, language, and emotion—into the task. *Commitment* is demonstrated through actions rather than words. However, the way we initiate *commitment* is through the making of a promise. Many people assume that everyone innately knows how to "be committed" to an activity or relationship, but *commitment* is a skill that must be learned, practiced, and developed. A large part of the transition years of adolescence are spent in learning this skill. For instance, a teenager may want to earn high marks and may be intelligent enough to do so, but if he or she is not able to remain committed to the studying it requires, the good grades will not come. Likewise, this happens in work situations when employees may desire to do a good job but may not have the emotional capacity that commits them to the needed actions. A personal example is someone who says, "I will quit smoking." After some time, we ask what he has done in relation to quitting, and he says, "Nothing. Still smoking." We might typically say that this person "is not committed"; however, ontologically we would say simply that he is more committed to smoking than not smoking. This is where it's important to understand that deep, sustainable learning happens cognitively, emotionally, and somatically. If the change has only been addressed in words—think New Year's resolutions—it won't occur, because there has been no shift in the emotional or somatic domains. Generally, people are blind to this and often fail to consider what they are committed to that keeps them from changing. Whenever we commit to something, we are freely choosing to focus on that thing and not on another. We are always committed to something, because our actions are not mechanical, so an important question is where our bigger commitment lies. Commitment is attention + energy.

■ **Compassion:** The emotion of *compassion* is often confused with *empathy, sympathy,* or *pity.* What is unique about compassion, if we take the meaning literally, is that it is the act of "being with another in their pain." It is the ability to completely be with someone who is struggling. In this interpretation, it does not require any other action. We do not need to help someone as we might when we feel *pity,* or we might not even be able to feel what they are feeling as in *empathy* or *sympathy.* Presence is the predisposition of *compassion.* This might seem passive, but actually people who experience deep *compassion* from another human being find that something in the way they see their breakdown changes after the encounter.

Compassion is the emotion that connects us with others and highlights our vulnerability and our dependence on our fellow humans. Compassion puts us to thinking that what is happening to the other at this time could happen to us in the future. Compassion is the emotion that demonstrates that we are unequivocally "interdependent," even if we'd prefer not to see it.

■ **Compliance:** *Compliance* means "I will do as you ask because I do not believe I have a choice." When we *comply*, we will take the action, but we will not do it with *commitment*. When you insist one of your children apologize to the other, this is often what you get. They will say the words "I'm sorry," but it is clear from their body language and their tone of voice that in fact they are not. As we grow up, we sometimes get a little better at this and will *comply* with rules at work or social standards without true commitment. Although full commitment is sometimes necessary, there are times when *compliance* is sufficient. For instance, when we drive on public streets, *complying* with the traffic laws is all we are asked to do. Its value as an emotion is that it gets people to act in consistent ways even when they do not fully understand why or agree that they need to. In essence, it can be seen as a streamlined way to generate aligned action.

■ **Confidence:** When I believe there is a strong probability that something will happen or get done, I am experiencing the emotion of *confidence*. It means "with fidelity." This allows me to move ahead without hesitation. It is similar to the emotion of trust, but derives from Latin roots rather than Northern European. As with *trust,* it is an assessment, and always includes risk. It is based on the belief that the other person is sincere, capable, and reliable to fulfill the task. When I have *self-confidence,* it demonstrates the belief that I will be successful at those things I choose to engage in.

■ **Confusion:** The American writer Henry Miller defined *confusion* in this way: "***Confusion is a word we have invented for an order which is not understood.***" Its root literally means "to pour together," which is a fair description of how it feels to us. The purpose of confusion is to point out that something we are experiencing does not fit into our understanding of the world. For instance, driving at night on the highway and seeing oncoming lights that appear to be in our lane. Our reaction is likely to be "What is going on?" or something of the sort. When a clerk gives us change for a purchase and it doesn't seem to add up to the correct total, we first experience *confusion.* So *confusion* is that stage where things "don't add up to how we understand the world." In these two scenarios we can see how it would protect us. In spite of this value, it is often labeled a "bad" emotion. When we are in learning situations, we start out understanding how the world works, the teacher shows us a new idea or model that does not fit our understanding, and *confusion* shows up as we try to integrate one with the other. Traditional education does not honor this moment of confusion as important, and in school many of us were chastised for "not being able to figure it out" or to quickly move beyond *confusion.* From those experiences we learn to see *confusion* as something to be avoided rather than a natural and predictable step in learning.

■ **Contentment:** Similar to feeling *satisfied*. A *contented* person's desires are "bound by what he or she already has," meaning there is no inclination to seek more, which would be the effect of *discontentment*. *Contentment* can be related to the material or relational aspects in life, or the more spiritual, much like *peace* and *serenity* are.

■ **Courage:** Our word courage comes from *coeur* or "heart" in French. Literally it means that we "have the heart to act even in the face of fear." That does not mean we will necessarily take action, but we could if we chose to. *Boldness* can be thought of as the emotion that allows us to act on our *courage*. Its relationship with *fear* makes *courage* a very individualized emotion. If you do not *fear* public speaking, you have no need for *courage* to present at a conference. If you do not have a *fear* of drowning, there is no need to have *courage* to swim in the ocean. If we listen closely to people, we will find those things they are *afraid* of when they speak about others acting *courageously*.

■ **Covetous:** To *covet* something is to have a passionate desire for it. The source of the word is the same as for Cupid, the Roman god of love. What it predisposes us to do is to look for ways to have the thing in our own life. Often we broaden covetousness to mean we want to take the thing we *covet* away from its owner. That would be true if there were only one of something in the world, but otherwise it is designed to alert us to what we feel passionate about having in life. If I covet the Hope Diamond, of course, the only way to satisfy my covetousness is to take possession of the Hope Diamond. However, the deeper message is that there is something about that particular diamond I desire. The same would be true of people. *Covetousness,* like *envy,* has been branded a "bad" emotion in its traditional interpretation, but can also be seen as a guide to our *passions* and *desires* in life. It all depends on how we listen to it.

■ **Curiosity:** "I believe there is something here of value to me, and I want to find out." *Curiosity* is the emotion that puts us into action investigating and asking questions in order to understand how a thing could be of value to us. If we remain *curious* for long enough without finding something that is of value to us, we may move into *boredom,* which is the opposite story: "I believe there is nothing here of value to me, so I will put my attention elsewhere." One of the principal values of *curiosity* is that by its nature it engages us with and immerses us in the world around us. Without it, we would live a very static existence.

■ **Cynicism:** *Cynicism* is almost always seen as a "negative" emotion and something to be avoided. It is sometimes considered an emotion of the elderly who have become jaded or a person who has suffered big disappointments in life. The root of *cynicism* has a history in itself. It is thought to have roots in the philosophical community of ancient Greece. The root word in Greek, *kynikos,* meant "a follower of Antisthenes," literally "doglike." Supposedly this came from the sneering sarcasm of his followers, but it's more likely from *Kynosarge,* "Gray Dog," the name of the gymnasium outside ancient Athens (for the use of those who were not pure Athenians) where the founder, Antisthenes, a pupil of Socrates, taught. Whether the source was the "doglike sneer" or not, this is the facial expression we associate with *cynicism.*

Cynicism can be thought of as a distrust of others' apparent good intentions. Because of that, it will always be found in opposition to emotions such as *enthusiasm* or *ambition.* Beyond distrust, *cynicism* moves one to "recruit others to our point of view." Someone speaking from this emotion will belittle others as *naïve* or blind. One unique quality of *cynicism* is its staying power. As long as a *cynic* can find or create opposition, he or she will feel powerful. That means that there is no rational argument that is likely to sway a *cynical* person, because that would mean they would have to give up their power. Underneath that resistance is a profound fear of becoming irrelevant or unimportant.

Cynicism should not be confused with *skepticism,* which exists to distinguish what we will believe from what we will not. In *cynicism* we are already strongly committed to what we believe is "realistic" or "possible" and are unwilling to consider changing that commitment. *Cynicism* challenges ungrounded *excitement* or *naiveté,* even though it may be harsh in its language and methods.

■ **Delight:** "To allure, charm, please, or entice" according to the Latin roots; it is the emotion that alerts us to an enjoyable surprise. Our reaction in *delight* is to feel lightness, and often we smile and clap our hands together. *Delight* can break us out of *boredom* or *seriousness* and give us unexpected moments of *joy.* It tells us something about what we do and don't expect in life and also what makes us *happy.*

■ **Denial:** *Denial* is generally thought of as a negative emotion, but it has its value. When we are in a grave or unbearable situation that we need to live through, it allows us to carry on. In *denial* our predisposition is to see only what we wish to see and to understand only what we want to understand. Everything outside of that ceases to exist. It can allow us tremendous focus and resolution. And, of course, these same attributes can blind us to things everyone else can see. Generally we can remain in *denial* until the crisis

68

deepens to the point that we have no choice but surrender. Addicts and people experiencing trauma may use *denial* in order to survive. Although it shows up quite differently, *denial* is similar to the emotion of *naiveté* in that it allows us to see the world in the way we wish it was rather than the way it is, and thus can be seen as contrasted with *acceptance*.

■ **Desire:** When you consider that the source of our word *desire* meant to "long for something that comes from the stars," you can feel its profound nature. A desire is a *yearning* or *longing*. If we listen to it, we will know what is most dear and important to us. When we think of our partner and feel *desire,* it is telling us how important they are to us. Although it can be and often is given a sexual interpretation, it can be applied to any part of life, even the most spiritual. Our predisposition in *desire* is to move closer to the person or object we yearn for.

■ **Despair:** To *despair* is "to lose all hope." It means that we cannot see future possibilities or perhaps even see a future at all. Our predisposition in *despair* is to give up trying. It differs from *resignation,* in which we also quit trying, but that is because we believe "Nothing we do will make a difference, so why try?" In *despair* we believe that there is not a difference to be made. It does not exist. The authors' personal experience of *despair* is that it, more than *sadness,* is the emotion most associated with depression. It is the inability to see any future possibilities that immobilizes us. The purpose of *despair* for human beings is a little mysterious but could be to help us move outside of ourselves to find support in a higher power. We might turn to nature or the universe or a single deity, but if we have lost all hope that we can cope individually, it forces us to look outside of ourselves for support.

■ **Dignity:** *Dignity* is one of the most important emotions in terms of self-identity, and yet it's often unfamiliar to people. To feel *dignity* means "to feel worthy." It is the belief that we are as important as any other person and that we deserve our place in the world. In other words, we are a legitimate human being. Another belief is that we have the right to choose for ourselves. When I am acting from dignity, I decide what I will believe, what I will do in my life, who I will be with, and what treatment I will accept from others. *Dignity* allows me to set my boundaries, and if they are crossed, *indignance* will be provoked to defend them. It is no surprise that most leaders of social movements embody *dignity* and insist on it as a basis for human interaction. Mandela, Gandhi, Martin Luther King, Mother Teresa, the Dalai Lama, along with a multitude of sociopolitical leaders have based their campaigns on the emotion of *dignity*. One inherent quality of this emotion is that if I embody *dignity,* I not only insist on it for myself but also must extend it to others, even those I am opposing. When we talk about someone who lacks "self-confidence," we are often speaking about a lack of *dignity.*

■ **Disappointment:** The emotion of *disappointment* arises when we realize that what we thought would happen and what is actually happening do not align. All humans appear to have the ability and even the need to imagine what the future will be like. We are continually building an expectation of what the future will look like. We expect it will be sunny or warm or that we will receive a project or a salary increase. Perhaps some of these things have been promised to us, but if not, they are simply our inventions of how we believe the future will be. When life behaves in a way that is *contrary* to our expectations, we experience the emotion of *disappointment*. Usually we think this *disappointment* means something is "wrong," when a more useful interpretation might be that our expectations and reality are simply misaligned. Life is not behaving as I expected it to. One thing that makes *disappointment* deeper is when we have become attached to our interpretation or expectation. That attachment generally will result in us resisting or *denying* what is becoming evident.

A misconception shows up when we say something like "I don't want to say no because I don't want to *disappoint* her." The underlying belief is that it is my action that generates the *disappointment* rather than the other person's expectations. In a case where I have made a promise, it has likely become part of the other person's expectations. If I promise my daughter to take her to the mall, then the idea of me taking her isn't just something she made up. Assuming she believed my promise and that she wanted to go to the mall, revoking it will probably generate *disappointment*. However, in other cases when someone promises something and doesn't deliver, I may be *relieved* rather than *disappointed*. If my brother-in-law promises to stop by on Sunday but I'd rather spend the day alone, I will feel *relieved* when he cancels.

■ **Disgust:** Literally "distasteful." When we say an experience "left a bad taste in my mouth," we are voicing *disgust*. When we taste something we dislike, our reaction is to spit it out, which is the predisposition of *disgust*. We want to get rid of or quit interacting with that person or situation. If a movie *disgusts* us, we will want to leave, and if we find another person's behavior *disgusting*, we will want it to stop or we will try to get away from it. *Disgust* tells us what we believe is "in good taste" or correct behavior and what is not. Although it is an emotion all humans share, the things we find *disgusting* depend highly on our individual and cultural makeup. Foods that are appreciated in one culture are considered *disgusting* in another. Public displays of affection likewise. In some cultures, nepotism is accepted and considered the norm, and in others it is thought of as *disgusting*. Individually we have developed our own lexicon of what will provoke *disgust*. For instance, if we are committed vegans, we may find the idea of eating meat *disgusting*. If we believe in self-control, someone who gets drunk at a party may provoke *disgust*. Feeling *disgust* does not equate to the thing or person being wrong, but rather informs us about our own beliefs and standards of behavior. It is very useful to understand this distinction because it informs us about ourselves, even when we often think it is telling us something about the other person.

■ **Dispassion:** More than any other emotion, *dispassion* is the one that allows us to come closest to "being objective." When we say we need to be objective, what we are saying is not that we need to eradicate emotions or be emotionless, but rather that we need to "put our emotions in neutral" so that we can leverage our reason as much as possible. *Dispassion* from the Greek literally means "to separate ourselves from passion or emotions." We could think of it as the other side of the coin from *compassion,* in which we are "being with the emotion or pain." In *dispassion* we are doing our best to act from a neutral place emotionally, even when it is not absolute.

■ **Doubt:** *Doubt,* as a sensation in the body, can feel somewhat similar to anxiety or fear. We can feel disconnected from the ground and it encourages us to hold back, thus slowing our movements and progress.

Doubt, however, means something very different from *fear* or *anxiety*. *Doubt* is letting me know that I am in new territory, and its message is to not take for granted that I am prepared. So it is logical for *doubt* to show up in any new activity or learning, since we will be in new territory. Doubt is a call to pay attention rather than a warning of impending problems. It is also predictable any time we are doing something new, learning something new, or acting in a new area of life.

Dread: Can you remember a time in your life when you were so afraid of something that you were immobilized? You couldn't get out of bed because of a situation you might face at work or you couldn't start a conversation you wanted and needed to have. In those moments, it is likely you were experiencing *dread*. *Dread* is warning us that something in the future may not just hurt us, but we believe it has the potential to destroy us. It is similar to *fear* and *anxiety* in terms of being a belief about the possibility of the future; it has some qualities of both, but is stronger than either.

Author's story (Dan): I can remember a period of several months when there was a breakdown with work that was being handled primarily through email. There were accusations and serious threats, some of which put my career in jeopardy and some of which threatened the future of an organization I was deeply committed to. Beyond the *anxiety* and *fear*, there was also *dread*, which I began to feel each time I opened my computer and checked my email, because each time I did, it seemed the crisis took a new turn and worsened. The *dread* I felt immobilized me at times, and I was unable to do something as simple as open my computer (so that I wouldn't have to face the next shock). My experience of the *dread* did not evaporate when the crisis ended, but took several months to fade.

- **Ease:** The emotion of *ease* is supported by tranquility of mind and an undisturbed body. That also pretty well describes our predisposition in *ease,* which is to be at peace and quiet and free from worry. This is an emotion that allows us to rest deeply and take a break from the concerns of the world.

- **Elation:** Literally "a lifting up," which is what we feel physically. Similar to *delight,* but stronger and with a different story. *Delight* is the response to a surprise we consider good, but *elation* has to do with satisfaction over one's accomplishments. We recognize and want to celebrate our good fortune and perhaps cannot imagine a better outcome. *Elation* could be evoked by achieving a challenging personal goal or by receiving accolades from others. It is similar to *pride* but is of greater energy, and with a desire to celebrate and not just tell others about our success.

- **Embarrassment:** Literally meaning "to block." In *embarrassment* our predisposition is to hide from others because of something we feel we have not done well or should not have done at all. It can be thought of as the opposite of *pride* in that sense. That does not make it morally wrong, but it is something we would prefer to keep private. *Embarrassment* contains an aspect of self-judgment in that we believe we "shouldn't be doing a certain thing" or that we "should" be able to do something better than we are. If we are *embarrassed* to speak a foreign language or play the piano publicly, it is because we have expectations higher than our competencies. It may have something to do with what we believe others' expectations are, but it largely has to do with our own. One thing *embarrassment* can show us is what things in life we aspire to be better at.

■ **Empathy:** Ontologically *empathy* means resonating with another's emotion to the degree that the emotion becomes our own. Sometimes we say we "take on" the emotion of the other. Because emotions are energies or vibrational in nature, it means we are aligning with the energy of the other person. *Empathy* is the emotion that tells other people we truly do understand the experience they are having. We each have a capacity for *empathy* that is part of our makeup, but it will be more available to us in situations where we have had experiences similar to the person we are with. For instance, someone who is a parent of a child with learning challenges may be more able to *empathize* with another parent in a similar situation. Someone who does not have that experience may be limited to *sympathy*, which means they can guess at the experience but do not have firsthand experience of it.

■ **Enchantment:** Our emotion enchantment comes from the Latin root *incantare*, which meant to "fix a spell upon." So when we feel *enchanted*, we are captivated by the event or person as in a way that seems magical.

■ **Enjoyment:** The emotion of *enjoyment* tells us we are experiencing something we find pleasant. Our predisposition therefore is to continue doing it or to do it again. Similar to *disgust, enjoyment* is highly individual. Some people *enjoy* hunting, while others *enjoy* knitting. We can *enjoy* being in a crowd of people, being alone, or both. The focus of *enjoyment* tends to be the present, although we may recall things we have *enjoyed* in the past or *anticipate enjoying* something in the future. *Enjoyment* stems from being in the current moment and does not require any outcome.

■ **Enthusiasm:** *Enthusiasm* comes from Greek roots and means to be "with the gods" or "with the divine." From this root idea we can understand *enthusiasm* as being connected with and committed to a cause greater than ourselves. This distinguishes it clearly from the emotion of *excitement,* which is a heightened level of energy but has no vision to sustain itself and can only be maintained with ever-higher levels of energy. Due to its connection with "something larger," enthusiasm has a durability and substance which *excitement* does not. It can also be distinguished from *ambition,* which is the emotion we experience when we see possibilities in life and are determined to take advantage of them. *Ambition* can be seen to be more focused on "obtaining or achieving something" and *enthusiasm* on "being in the service of something."

In organizations, this larger care is generally represented in the vision and/or mission statements. The power of *enthusiasm* for leaders is that it can give them sustained energy and direction, particularly when times are trying. It can help them speak about their vision so that others can also see a new possibility for the future, and this gives direction to their work. For employees, this connection with a greater cause means they do not need to rely only on the leader for *inspiration.* If or when the leader leaves the organization or acts out of alignment with the vision, it can still be their guide. It's essential that a leader understand the difference between generating *excitement,* acting with *ambition,* and eliciting *enthusiasm,* in order to direct his or her team effectively.

■ **Entitlement:** *Entitlement* literally means "to have title to" or "to own." It is connected with the story that I deserve something. This can manifest in a couple of different ways. One way it shows up is in the idea that "the world owes me," and this is the *entitlement* we often see in adolescents or when we think someone is "spoiled." Another way is in its similarity with *dignity* in that, "as a human being, I have the right for certain things to be my choice." The entitlement meaning "I believe the world owes me" is often a source of suffering and causes suffering. It is often part of *resentment* and can underlie *resignation*. It also stands in opposition to *gratitude,* in which one believes that everything they are and have is a gift. Careful listening is required to distinguish which "entitlement" is being expressed.

Envy: *Envy* is another emotion we generally label "bad." It is among the cardinal sins and is often defined as not just *jealousy* of what another person is or has, but the desire to take it away from them. Sometimes this is referred to as *malicious envy*. If we look at simple *envy*, we would interpret it as "the desire to have what another has." In this way it can be useful to listen to it, as it can help us understand what we believe is missing from our lives. If we *envy* another person's job or house, what it is trying to tell us is that there is something about that job or house that we would like to have in our own lives. *Envy* does not necessarily include the desire to take "it" away from the other person, which would be *resentment* ("it shouldn't be this way") or *revenge* ("desire to get even"). *Envy* is one of several strong emotions which we have difficulty allowing ourselves to experience. Many people feel *shame* or *embarrassment* that they are *envious*. As a result, they don't have the opportunity to reflect on what *envy* is trying to communicate, because they immediately try to hide it. Listening to *envy* can help us set our sights on creating a life that satisfies us. In this interpretation it is far from a "bad" emotion.

■ **Equanimity:** *Equanimity* means to consider things calmly and evenly, giving equal weight to all. Its predisposition is to consider without prejudice, and it is the emotion that allows us to come closest to what we refer to as objectivity. It means "an even mind or spirit."

■ **Eroticism:** The word *erotic* provokes strong reactions. In the West, we associate eroticism with sex and sex acts. It is true that the Greek root *Eros* did mean "sexual love," but *eroticism* can have a much broader meaning that is connected with *passion*. *Passion* derives from a root that includes "suffering, enduring, and desiring." Ontologically, *eroticism* is "the desire, longing, or yearning to become one with an object of desire." That could be a person, but could also be art, music, nature, spirit, or other aspects of the world we consider profoundly attractive. When the so-called "whirling dervishes" of the Sufi danced, it was considered to be an *erotic* act, and *eroticism* is a part of all the arts. Whichever interpretation one uses, it is important to remember that although there is a predisposition in every emotion, it does not mean we must take that action. We can feel *eroticism* without acting on it, but it can nonetheless inform us of what we *yearn* for.

■ **Euphoria:** *Euphoria* is "the recognized experience of extraordinary well-being." It is an emotion that is very attractive to most people. It can be provoked by ritual and practice but is also the emotion that makes some drugs and activities addictive. In a sense it is the opposite of *hopelessness,* because in *euphoria* anything and everything seems possible. When we talk about oscillating between mania and depression, we are probably talking about the emotions of *euphoria* and *despair.* The purpose of *euphoria* could be to give us the experience

78

of how extraordinary the world can be, to show us the upper limit of our experiences.

- **Excitement:** From the Latin *exciere*, to "call forth, instigate," from *ex-* "out" + *ciere* "set in motion, call." *Excitement* is the emotion that gets us moving or into action. Interestingly, *excitement* doesn't have a direction of its own, which can sometimes be problematic. A highly *excited* child in a religious service or an excited employee in a focused planning meeting may not be helpful or productive because the *excitement* is not aligned with the context.

- **Exhilaration:** Our word hilarious derives from the same roots and gives a sense of its predisposition—to laugh wildly, to be cheerful, to be merry. To be *exhilarated* is to be very, very happy to the point of not being able to contain the emotional energy, hence the laughter.

- **Exuberance:** The story of *exuberance* is that we believe the world is overflowing with abundance. While *hopeful* means we believe there are possibilities in life, *exuberance* means we believe life is fruitful. When we believe this, we are inclined to indulge, appreciate, and share with others all that is available.

- **Faith:** While reason could be defined as "belief based on evidence," *faith* could be thought of as "belief without the need for evidence." The root of *faith* is the Latin *fidere*, which means "to trust." Ontologically we would say that reason is what allows us to have beliefs in the material world, where it is possible to produce visible evidence, and that *faith* is its counterpart in the immaterial world, and that is its purpose.

■ **Fascination:** Like so many other emotions, the source of our word *fascination* is Latin. It meant to "enchant or charm," and that is the experience it gives us. We are riveted by something or someone and place all our attention on it or them. It is as if that person or thing has cast a spell upon us. *Fascination* does not require that we understand why we are interested; in fact, not knowing may make it all the more attractive. The value of having *fascination* in our repertoire of emotions is that it allows us to focus intently.

■ **Fear:** *Fear* is a warning of possible future harm, and it tells us exactly what the source might be. If we are afraid of losing our job or failing in the eyes of our team, we know the source of the *fear*. Being injured in an auto accident, betrayed by a friend, or losing our wallet could be sources of *fear*. Traditionally we have believed that *fear* meant something bad "is going to happen," when actually what it is telling us is to pay attention to what might harm us so that we have the opportunity to remove the threat. *Fear* can then be seen as a very useful and even friendly emotion that helps us take care of ourselves by anticipating and avoiding potential dangers.

■ **Forgiveness:** *Forgiveness* is an emotion many people wrestle with, because traditionally we have understood it as something we do for the other person, and also because we believe it needs to include forgetting. To *forgive* means that "I remember the injury you caused me, but I will not use it to punish you in our future interactions." If we forget the injustice, *forgiveness* is not necessary, so remembering what happened is essential. It also does not mean I've changed my mind about the belief that you hurt me; it simply means I won't use it against you in the future. The purpose of *forgiveness* is to free ourselves so that we can continue to interact and not to let the other person off the hook. *Forgiveness* as an emotion must be practiced in order to be mastered. I may say I *forgive* a certain deed, but in the future when I recall what occurred, I will almost certainly need to renew my commitment to *forgiveness*. By doing this over time, my thinking may become more habitual, but will still need renewing. *Forgiveness* can be offered by the person wronged or it can be requested by the offender, but in either case, the outcome can be to free both.

Frustration: The story of *frustration* is that "it should have happened already." It could also be that "it shouldn't have happened," but it's always one or the other. *Frustration* occurs because humans have the unique capacity to generate a story of how we believe the future will be. That is called an expectation. Expectations come from two sources. When someone we trust promises us something by a certain time, we generally expect that thing to happen at that time. If it does not occur, we may feel *frustration* because "it should have already happened." Another place expectations come from is our own inventive thinking. In every moment, whether we are aware of it or not, we are creating a story of how the next minute, hour, day, year, or lifetime will be. A lot of this is based on what has happened in the past. We live in the story that when we put the keys in the ignition of our car, it will start, that a friend will invite us to his birthday party, or that it will be a sunny day tomorrow. When the thing we thought would occur doesn't, there is a moment when we realize that life is not happening the way we imagined it. In that moment we experience *disappointment* and can also experience *frustration*. *Disappointment* tells us that there

81

is a misalignment between our story of life and how life is behaving. *Frustration* is the story that that shouldn't happen. We often think that because we are *frustrated,* something is "wrong," when in fact it is just informing us that something doesn't meet our standards or expectations. *Frustration* and *anger* are sometimes used interchangeably, but while *anger* has to do with a perceived injustice, *frustration* stems from unfulfilled expectations.

■ **Fury:** Meaning "a violent passion, madness, or rage"—Latin *furia. Fury* is the emotion that allows us to attack or defend ourselves without concern for the consequences. In moments of desperation, it may be what allows us to survive. It is similar to *rage* in its energy, but the focus is different. *Fury* is provoked by care of ourselves or a cause, while *rage* is the impulse to destroy because we do not feel any care or believe there is any good in that which we are attacking. If you were to observe a parent trying to protect their child from a wild animal, you would be seeing the emotion of *fury.* The attacking is not to destroy the animal *(rage)* or because of *anger* (the animal is unjustly attacking the child), but *fury* to defend what they care about without concern for their own well-being.

■ **Generosity:** Meaning "magnanimous" or "of noble birth." Although magnanimity isn't a word we use often, it literally means "great-souled," so the implication is that someone in the mood of *generosity* would be inclined to give to others without expecting anything in return. *Generosity* then is the emotion from which we give gifts, but if there is the expectation of something in return, it is not pure. The value of this emotion is that it allows us to give to others without attachment. It doesn't necessarily mean that we have more than others or that they are in need or that we *pity* them, only that we want to share what we have.

- **Gratitude:** The root of the word *gratitude* is related to the Latin *gratis*, "for free." *Gratitude* is the emotion we feel when we have received something for free or as a gift. In its largest sense, *gratitude* is the belief that all that we are and all that happens in our lives are gifts. In other words, we didn't earn this life, but it was given to us by a creator, the universe, or evolution. That is what we are saying in a ritualized way when we say grace before dinner. Of all the emotions, *gratitude* may be the one we have the greatest ability to choose and embrace. By declaring that we will learn this emotion, we can shift a life lived in the mood of *entitlement* to one lived in *gratitude*.

- **Gravitas:** The emotion of *gravitas* allows us to consider things seriously. In certain contexts, we consider this emotion to be more *trustworthy* than other emotions. For instance, a banker that is not able to bring some *gravitas* to interactions will likely not be trusted as much as one that can. In scientific research, it is an emotion that serves to keep the focus on serious, thoughtful study.

- **Greed:** *Greed* comes from Old English, meaning to be "hungry" or "voracious." As an emotion, it can be understood as a permanent condition of hunger, and thus we will continue to take whether we need it or not. So the predisposition of *greed* is simply to take all that it can get. The emotion that balances *greed* is *satisfaction,* which is the recognition that "I have enough." One way of navigating *greed* is to declare "conditions of satisfaction." That is, "What conditions would exist that would allow me to say I have enough?" Greed is one emotion that allows us to gather harvests and store them when we do not currently need the food (although *prudence* could also motivate us to do that). It allows us to consider preserving food or building financial security for retirement; however, its shadow is that it doesn't have anything limiting it unless we have developed complementary emotions. One of those is *satisfaction*.

Our current economic situation, where there are people with far more than will produce *satisfaction* and yet they continue to accumulate, is a result of *greed*. Societally we have cast this as a moral issue, and we often classify *greed* in that way. But ontologically we would say that we have learned the emotion of *greed* and now it has become habitual, meaning we do not stop to think what it means and what is our relationship with it. If the human world is to become more egalitarian, it will only do so when we learn more about how the emotion of *greed* lives in each of us.

- **Grief:** *Grief* comes from Latin *gravare*, which meant "make heavy; weighty." These are a good description of the feelings we have in this emotion. *Grief* is often connected to the emotion of *sadness,* because in that emotion we feel that life is difficult and toilsome, but *grief* stands on its own. The opportunity grief gives us is to appreciate when life is moving more smoothly, to sometimes slow down to a step-by-step process, and also to request the support of others. It does not necessarily make us less independent, but can encourage us to develop interdependence.

- **Guilt:** *Guilt* feels bad. It makes us feel small or less than other people. The point of this feeling is to get our attention, because *guilt* plays an essential role in helping us see our personal values. Guilt shows up when we have violated one of our values. If we did not feel *guilt,* we would not be aware we had transgressed our standards and would not be able to see the boundaries of our beliefs. In this sense *guilt* is essential in order to understand ourselves. If we feel *guilty* when we do not keep a promise, even a small one, it tells us that we see our promises as important. If we feel *guilty* when we pass a beggar on the street without giving them something, it means we believe it is our responsibility to help people in need. If we feel *guilt* when we do not tell the whole truth, it lets us know that we believe this is incorrect behavior. *Guilt* is another case where we've labeled an emotion as "bad" when in fact it provides us with essential information and is the basis for our identity.

An important intrinsic element of *guilt* is that it sometimes has invisible standards that we have learned. We often express these as "should" or "shouldn't." We often think of these standards as ethical, as in "should = correct behavior" and "shouldn't = incorrect behavior," but because *guilt* reveals personal beliefs, these "shoulds" and "shouldn'ts" are highly individual. They look like universal values to us, but they have often been adopted from our families or culture for the purpose of guiding our personal behavior. More universal "shoulds" and "shouldn'ts" are connected with the emotion of *shame.*

Happiness: Late 14c., "lucky, favored by fortune, prosperous"; of events, "turning out well," from *hap,* "chance, fortune" + *-y.* Thus *happiness* is the emotion co-creative with the story that "things are turning out well" for me or that I am "fortunate." The implication is that there is not a fixed set of circumstances that will elicit *happiness,* but happiness is up to my interpretation. I could be *happy* I find money in the street because it means to me that I am fortunate. Another person may not experience *happiness* at the same turn of events. A certain job, relationship, or possession could "make me *happy*" depending on my assessment of being fortunate to have that job, that relationship, or that possession. The U.S. Declaration of Independence says that "the pursuit of *happiness*" is one of the unalienable rights of all human beings. It does not say we have the right to be *happy,* but only to pursue a life in which we believe "things are turning out well and we are fortunate."

■ **Hate:** The root of *hate* is very old and is connected with "sorrow." Beyond that, we do not know much about its origin. We often think of it as the opposite of *love,* but etymologically it seems more closely connected with *sadness,* which means "having had one's fill" or "being weary of." Perhaps a fitting meaning is that when we say we *hate* something or someone, we are saying we have had our fill and are done with it or them. We no longer want to associate or engage with it or them. This explains a lot in terms of our desire to get away from people or situations we *hate.* There is nothing inherent in the ontological interpretation of *hate* that would make us want to harm another. In *anger* we are predisposed to punish and in *rage* to destroy, and those emotions in association with hate are what give it its sometimes violent interpretation. The predisposition of *hate* is simply to "be away" from the thing or person and to not have any connection or association with it or them.

■ **Helpless:** To help means to "support, succor; benefit, do good to; cure, amend." When we are living the story that we are unable to do those things, we are experiencing the emotion of *helplessness.* When we feel *helpless,* we will not act because we do not believe we are able to have an impact on the situation. It could be that we believe we cannot help ourselves, or it could be the belief that we cannot help others. As is the case with other emotions, it may not be true that we cannot change the situation, but we truly believe that is the case.

Honor: From Latin, meaning "dignity, office or reputation." It is the emotion that allows us to protect our reputation. When what we have done is under attack, it provides the energy for us to take a stand to defend our action. *Honor* as an emotion is concerned with taking actions that defend what we believe is "right" even when others may not believe those actions are ethical. A soldier that sacrifices him- or herself for a comrade may also be acting out of *honor.*

Hope: "To look forward," "to wish for," or "to expect" are ways of articulating the emotion of *hope.* It is evident from this that the time orientation of *hope* is the future, and a future we desire. Generally, *hope* means we see the possibility of a future that is as good as or better than our present. The predisposition of *hope* is to make plans and consider possibilities that will help usher in the future we desire. As an emotion, *hope* provides us with the energy to move forward even when we may be in difficult circumstances. *Hope* and *expectancy* have things in common, although there is more attachment to our vision of the future when we are *expectant.* Either can be the root of *disappointment,* which is the realization that our vision of the future is not going to come to pass.

Hopelessness: As with other emotions, our word *hopeless* derives from Old English, while *despair* comes from Latin and could be thought of as the same emotion. They describe the same story of being unable to see a positive future and have the same predisposition of listlessness.

■ **Horror:** "To bristle with fear or terror." We experience *horror* when what we encounter is as bad as we can imagine. Physically we experience "a shaking, trembling, shudder, or chill" and desire to get away or avoid the experience. Knowing how bad things can be allows us to appreciate safety and security. *Horror* can also protect us from truly destructive activities.

■ **Hubris:** *Hubris* has the powerful origin in Greek of meaning "presumption toward the gods." In other words, someone acting from *hubris* imagines themselves as above other humans and being godlike. From that belief arise actions that are imprudent and lead to a fall when the person is revealed to be human after all. Hubris surpasses *arrogance,* which just means to think of yourself as better or morally superior to other people. The value of *hubris* is that it helps us understand the limits of our humanity, which is what makes it so attractive as the moral of many classic stories.

■ **Humiliation:** *Humiliation* means "to be *humbled*"; that is, to be reminded of what and who we are. The *embarrassment* or *shame* we feel in *humiliation* is connected with the fact that we have pretended to be more than we are in some way and now realize we are not. We often say someone "*humiliated* me," but it is we who have presumed to be more than we are and have thus created the situation. The other person has simply revealed the truth. *Humiliation* as an emotion keeps us aware of our abilities and limits.

■ **Humility:** This is an emotion with a very strong traditional interpretation that the authors do not find useful. We often think "to be *humble*" means to put ourselves below or to think of ourselves as less than others. That is the story we would assign to the emotion *obsequiousness*. A more useful interpretation of *humility* is "claiming all that we are and nothing that we are not." In other words, *humility* is a grounded sense of self. The Latin root means "of the earth," which is consistent with this interpretation. This way of thinking about it has made *humility* a powerful emotion for helping people develop their sense of self-worth and dignity. It also means that one is constantly striving to align oneself with one's true capabilities, skills, and characteristics. This leads to the sense in others that we are sincere and are not hiding anything or pretending to be what we are not. *Humility* can be thought of as an absence of pretense. One opportunity this interpretation opens up is that *pride* is no longer inconsistent with *humility*. When we do something we believe is good and want to share it, we can be at ease feeling *pride,* knowing we are not bragging or pretending to be more than we are or claiming more than we have done.

- **Impatience:** *Impatience* literally means "the refusal to submit or be lenient." In other words, when we are *impatient* we are standing our ground in terms of our standards. That does not automatically mean that our standards are logical or helpful, but if we listen to our *impatience,* we will know how we think life "should" be lived. In this interpretation *impatience* is closer to *indignance* than *anger*. *Impatience* does not imply there is anything unjust, only that there is something I won't accept according to my standards. From that we can see that it is useful to us to insist on and maintain the standards we believe best.

- **Incredulity:** Something "not worthy to be believed" or "too good to be true." If incredulity were pure, we would stop there and not believe, but in some situations we try to convince ourselves it "could" be true, which could be *euphoria* coming into play. Buying lottery tickets or being involved in a Ponzi scheme are two examples. The value of *incredulity* is that it forces us to look for evidence that something is indeed true rather than being *naïve* and believing it just because we would like life to be that way.

■ **Indifference:** The emotion *indifference* is exactly what it sounds like. It is the state in which we do not care if one thing or another happens. It does not make a difference to us. It is an emotion that allows us to follow others without resistance or submit to authority. It differs from *resignation* in that we know we could choose, but don't believe the outcome will be significantly better or worse for us either way. We might contrast *indifference* with *care,* in which it does make a difference to us what is decided.

■ **Indignation:** It might seem that if *dignity* means I believe I am worthy, *indignation* might mean I do not believe I am worthy. In the world of emotions, though, *indignation* is the emotion that is provoked when someone treats me as if I am unworthy when I believe I am. To be *indignant* means to "defend my boundaries and not allow others to treat me in ways I believe crosses them." *Indignation* can be confused with *anger,* as they feel similar. There is rising energy and narrowing focus. Sometimes we raise our voices, but the story of the two emotions is very different. *Anger* carries the predisposition to punish because we think the other person has done something unjust. *Indignance* is the predisposition to take care of ourselves because we believe the other person is crossing a boundary. *Anger* is focused on the other, while *indignance* is focused on ourselves. Because *anger* is a very popular emotion and *indignance* largely unknown, we tend to confuse the two. If we learn that *anger* is dangerous or shameful and thus avoid it, we will not have access to the one emotion we can call upon to take care of ourselves, *indignance*.

■ **Irreverence:** *Irreverence* gives us the ability to challenge or question what is sacrosanct. It means that we do not feel *awe* or *fear* of something that other people do. It allows us to think outside traditional limits. Political satire or poking fun at authority through irony falls into the category of irreverence. It could also be the emotion that allows someone to break tradition in art in order to invent a new artistic movement. *Irreverence* then becomes an emotion that fuels creativity and innovation because the previous limits are not allowed to limit new thinking. It is not the same as *disrespect*, because it does not oppose traditional beliefs but simply disregards them in order to pursue something new.

■ **Jealousy:** *Jealousy* can be thought of as the fear of losing something we care about, although many times it is not a "something" but a "someone." Since we can only lose possession of something we own, the underlying illusion of most *jealousy* is that the "someone" belongs to me. In that case, my reaction becomes to try to "hold on" to what I am afraid of losing. The results of this interpretation are legion, and in its most intense forms leads to the idea that "If I can't have it/him/her, then no one will."

However, *jealousy* can be listened to differently. We can hear its message that there is something or someone we care about very much, and it can be a reminder to consider whether we are attending to the

91

relationship. Does that person understand their importance to us? Are we putting as much effort into the relationship as we truly want? If we understand that in reality nothing and no one belongs to us, we will see that actually we are powerless to compel another, and the only option is to be as attractive as we are able. *Jealousy* is one of the emotions in which *responding* is frequently more effective than *reacting*.

■ **Joy:** *Joy* occurs when we experience something that is pleasurable or that makes us happy. It has a sense of serene well-being, and the predisposition of *joy* is to allow the experience to remain and to appreciate it while it continues.

■ **Judgmental:** When we think *judgmentally*, it is because we believe that our opinion carries some authority to say what is right and what is wrong. If we have been granted the authority to *judge* a situation or person, this may be true, but many times we confuse *assessing* with *judging*. An *assessment* is an interpretation of the value of something, and it is true to us but not universally true. A *judgment*, when we have the authority to issue it, does define a universal truth. For instance, if it is our role as a judge to declare a person's innocence or guilt, our *judgment* determines the future for all involved. When employed deliberately with purpose and care, *judgment* is an essential emotion.

■ **Loneliness:** This emotion and the following one are often confused, but it is enormously valuable to understand the difference. Both have to do with being alone, but in one we do not feel complete and in the other our completeness is not determined by the company of others. *Loneliness* means that we are alone and we believe that means we are incomplete. The predisposition then would be to seek out someone to complete us. It is likely that even when we find someone to share life with, we will continue to feel incomplete if we remain in this emotion.

■ **Lonesomeness:** When we are alone and yet feel complete, we are in the emotion of *lonesomeness*. The story is that we are complete whether we are with others or only in our own company. In *lonesomeness,* wholeness isn't a function of others being part of our life. Its predisposition is to move through life as we choose in contentment, and if we encounter others we enjoy being with, it will be a lovely surprise, but our happiness does not depend on it. This emotion could be thought of as "glass half-full," whereas *loneliness* is a "glass half-empty."

■ **Love:** There are perhaps more words written about this emotion than any other, and there are thousands of interpretations and variations. For the purposes of this book, we are using the interpretation that *love* exists when we "accept the other person as a fully legitimate human being." It is strongly related to *dignity, respect,* and *gratitude.* Romantic *love* then would be a relationship where we have no desire to change the other person, but accept them as the gift they are. It is worth noting the difference between liking someone, which means we enjoy spending time with them, and love. We believe we can *love* someone even when we do not *like* them or something they do, or approve of their choices. This is what allows a parent to care for his or her children even when the child is rebellious, disobedient, or simply independent.

■ **Loyalty:** Loyalty is the emotion that allows us to recognize and care for a group of which we believe we are a part. Its predisposition is to defend that group and its boundaries. *Loyalty* can be attached to many different entities. We can be *loyal* to a belief, a partner, a political party, a leader, a nation, an organization, or ourselves, which creates the potential of conflicting loyalties. It is not unusual for *loyalty* to be the reason people defend things that do not make sense to us as outside observers.

■ **Lust:** From Old English, *lust:* "desire, appetite, pleasure; sensuous appetite." This interpretation has not changed much, although lust has become more associated with sex than food. The predisposition of *lust* is to take and enjoy without concern for the consequences. Experiencing *lust* informs us of what we "have an appetite for" or what we desire. As with other emotions, *lust* does not dictate that we will indulge ourselves, but is a pointer to what we would like to do.

■ **Mischievous:** Constructed as the opposite of "achieve," *mischievous* literally means "bring to a head," and it implies trouble, harm, and misfortune. Over time the meaning has evolved to be lighter and to describe troublemaking rather than just trouble. The predisposition of *mischievous* is to trick or fool people into thinking something is wrong when it is not. It is an emotion that allows us to be playful and break the mood of an overly serious situation.

■ **Naiveté:** The emotion associated with innocence, *naiveté* means "natural" or "innate" and can be thought of as our level of emotional competence when young. Ontologically we are living in the story that "the world should be the way I would like it to be." If we are resentful that we were laid off from a company even though we knew the economy and company were in difficult straits, we may be in *denial,* but we may also have blinded ourselves out of *naiveté*. Out of this emotion we often complain about how things are in life, not because we have any grounds that they "should" be different, but only because we believe life should be the way we want it to be. Ultimately *naiveté* can take a lot of our energy, because we are constantly encountering life as it is when we believe it should be otherwise. The benefit of *naiveté* is that it allows us to be very open to the possibility of goodness, simplicity, or justice in ways that other emotions cannot.

■ **Nostalgia:** When people talk about "the good old days," they are generally speaking from *nostalgia*. In *nostalgia* we are thinking that "the past was better than the present, and I would like to go back." It is an emotion whose time orientation is definitely the past. The purpose of *nostalgia* is not for us to go backward in time but to recall those things that were meaningful in the past and consider how we could generate something similar in our current or future life. When *nostalgia* is a mood, we cannot be present, and we also have difficulty creating the future because we are always trying to re-create the past.

■ **Obligation:** To feel *obligated* means "to be aware of those things I must do." The list of things can be based on our promises and commitments, on societal or cultural expectations, or on our values. As an emotion, *obligation* keeps us focused on taking actions even when we may not feel inclined to do so at the moment. We often say, "I have to x," which is a clear indicator of this emotion. Although we may have freely committed to something we later see as *obligatory*, we generally do not feel *freedom* alongside *obligation*.

- **Optimism:** *Optimism* means "I know that good things and bad things happen, but mostly good things happen to me." In this it differs from *naiveté*, which blinds us to the bad things in life. The purpose of *optimism* is to allow us to move ahead freely in life because we believe the odds are in our favor. It may be that something bad will happen, but probably not.

- **Passion:** Late Latin *passionem*, "suffering, enduring." From the root, it is clear that it is a profound emotion experientially. An ancient use of *passion* is embodied in the concept of "the *passion* of Christ" or other religious contexts. We sometimes say someone "suffers for their art." Like *eroticism*, however, our modern interpretation is often connected with sex, although more broadly it means "a profound desire to be as close as possible to someone or something we yearn for." This is one of the emotions that allow us to pursue activities or relationships with a singular focus and to set aside *doubt,* exhaustion, or fatigue. If you imagine *passion* as the fuel for a mountain climber, you can imagine it helping supersede any obstacle. Likewise in pursuing a relationship, in painting, music, or other pursuits.

- **Peace:** The origin of *peace* is Latin for "absence of war, treaty, or tranquility." It means that we are emotionally at rest and not fighting *doubt, fear,* or *anxiety.* The human concern it takes care of is allowing us to rest without tension. We can infer from its roots that it is something we can declare if we need to rest. We can make an agreement with others or we can choose for ourselves moments of *peace.*

- **Persistence:** "To continue steadfastly." When we are in the emotion of *persistence,* we will continue to try a thing until it succeeds. It can be invaluable in a situation where we are doing the right thing but have not yet succeeded. In that sense, it is somewhat the opposite of *frustration*. The shadow of *persistence* is that we can, as the saying goes, "continue hitting our head against the wall" without any results. There is a distinction between *persistence* ("to keep trying") and *rigor*, which means to choose a form and maintain it. In the first, our energy is outwardly focused on the result of what we are doing, and in the latter, we are focused internally on the way we are doing it.

■ **Pessimism:** "I know that good things and bad things happen in life, but mostly bad things happen to me." *Pessimism* comes from a root that means "bottommost," which makes it quite clear. The value of *pessimism* is that it allows us to consider what may go wrong or what bad thing may happen. It turns our attention to that area rather than ignoring the possibility, as we might in *optimism*. As a mood, it may keep us from acting, because it has some of the qualities of *resignation*, but as an emotion it can help us make *prudent* choices that take in the full range of possible outcomes.

■ **Pity:** *Pity* means that "I recognize the suffering of others but look down on them because I am in some way superior." In other words, I believe they need my help. *Pity* can be appropriate in a case where I do, in fact, have superior capability or resources. When I see an animal that has been hit by an automobile and feel *pity*, it is because I rightly recognize its suffering, I do have superior capabilities, and it does need my help. But *pity* can also have a quality of inferring that the sufferer is less important than I am, which results in condescension. When we *pity* other human beings, it can sometimes be for this reason.

Author's story (Dan): In my 30s I co-led a choir for women with intellectual disabilities. After a time, I realized that one of the emotions out of which I was acting was *pity*. I believed I had superior capabilities and they needed my help. On one level, this was true. I knew the music and how to organize the singers. However, over time I realized that in the domain of experiencing and practicing *joy*, they far surpassed me. They sang *joyously* whether they knew the words, were in tune, or could follow the rhythm. Always. It was a *humbling* realization that at the same time I might be feeling *pity* for their limitations, they could just as easily have been feeling *pity* for me for my limited ability to experience *joy*. For that I needed their help.

■ **Pride:** *Pride* is another of the cardinal sins, but a close reading of linguistic translation reveals that the word in its original language was closer to what we now define as *arrogance.* Ontologically *pride* means that "I have done something I believe is good and I want to tell others about it." If I get a raise, pass an exam, score a goal, or cook a dinner that I believe is good and want to tell others about it, I am feeling *pride*. I can also feel *pride* in others, as we do when our children do something well. *Pride* allows us to share our accomplishments so that others can know what we value accomplishing in life. If we believe that makes us superior to others, we are lapsing into *arrogance,* but *pride* is simply designed to tell others what we think is good about who we are or what we are doing.

Author's story (Dan): I once worked with a young woman who appeared to me to be quite successful at most things she did and was very likable. She complained that she did not feel close in her relationships and thought there was something wrong with her that others did not like. Through our coaching, what was revealed was her lack of distinction between *pride* and *arrogance*. She had learned it was wrong to talk about her accomplishments, because that was *arrogant*. The cost of that was it did not allow her to share the things she was proud of, and as a consequence put a barrier up in all her relationships. In one way, it prevented others from knowing her. Once she embraced the difference and practiced the different conversations, she found that she could share those things that made her *proud,* which had a profound impact on the depth of her relationships.

Prudence: When you walk into a dark room you are not familiar with, how do you proceed? It is unlikely that you run in at full speed. More likely you move step by step, feeling your way along as you go. This is *prudence* in action. In thought and decision-making, it means to "think ahead," "foresee the consequence," and "decide wisely." Just as with walking into a dark room, *prudence* allows us to move step by step and with foresight, so that we don't injure ourselves or create undesirable situations.

Rage: *Rage* is included in this list not so much because we individually experience it often, but because it is something we see in media reports, and it can be a little difficult to work out how it is not a "bad" emotion. How could *rage* be a benefit or give humans the ability to do something they could not without it? Rage is associated with killing, with war, and with unthinking destruction. What occurred during the French Revolution or the genocide in Rwanda or during the Second Gulf War in the days after the U.S. Army entered Baghdad are examples of destruction for its own sake. Crimes of passion are often attributed to *rage.* The emotion of *rage* is co-creative with the story that "nothing is worth saving," and the predisposition is to destroy. It is often thought of as an extreme anger, but actually has a different underlying story and disposition and is thus a unique emotion. It is tempting to think that *rage* is an emotion available only to others who have the capacity, but from personal experience the authors would say that it is available to each of us if the circumstances are right.

■ **Regret:** *Regret* is an emotion that seems to be about the past, but can be thought of as a guide to the future. The story we are living in *regret* is that "life would be better if I had or hadn't done x." That story presupposes something we cannot know. It could be true, but life could have also turned out worse. Something to consider is that we sometimes say we "should have made a different decision," but upon examination we can see that given how we saw the world and understood our options at the moment of decision, we could not have, which means our regret is generally groundless. That does not mean it is without value; we simply need to look a bit deeper for which human concern *regret* takes care of. What purpose does it have for us? One possibility is that *regret* is trying to guide us in future decisions. If we feel *regret* that we did not call a friend during their time of difficulty, perhaps it is inviting us to be more attentive to this in the future. If we *regret* spending money in a particular way, it is inviting us to look at how we make those choices. So the purpose of *regret,* far from just making us "feel bad," is to enhance our awareness and wisdom.

■ **Remorse:** The story that generates the emotion of *remorse* is that "what I did was wrong." It doesn't necessarily include the reason why I believe this, only that I now believe it was incorrect behavior. Generally, we believe it was wrong because it violated our personal values or the values of a community we are part of. This is why *remorse* often occurs alongside *guilt* (violating our own standards) or *shame* (violating the standards of the community). The primary purpose of *remorse* is to get our attention to look at how we have been acting out of alignment personally or culturally, and to allow us to communicate that to others.

- **Resentment:** *Resentment* means I believe that what is occurring or has occurred was not fair to me. For instance, "I shouldn't have to work past age 60," "I shouldn't have been fired," or "I work hard all week, so I deserve to have good weather on the weekend." Or it means life should be different in my favor: "I should have a bigger house," or "They should appreciate me more." The primary focus is unfairness. It is my belief that something in life isn't as it should be, and that is unfair to me. *Resent* literally means "to feel again," and that is the experience we have as the same thoughts of unfairness return over and over. Although we can get caught by and stuck in these thoughts, the main purpose of resentment is to help us distinguish what we believe is fair from what we believe is not fair. From there we can take steps to either understand differently or to correct what we believe needs to be corrected. Without *resentment*, we would not know where to start. All social reformers are moved by *resentment*, because they perceive something is unfair in the status quo and are unwilling to accept it.

- **Resignation:** To *resign* from a job means that we "give it up." Basically *resignation* is the emotion in which we give up hope and power. It is living the story that "nothing I do will make any difference, so why try?" Although often seen as a very negative emotion, it also has a very useful purpose. The reason we might give up a job is that it is exhausting and we need to rest. *Resignation* as an emotion allows us to do just that, because its predisposition is to withdraw ourselves from effort. As a mood, it will mean we live life without attempting to shape it as we would like and will have no choice in what happens.

- **Respect:** To *respect* means to have a high regard for something or someone and consider them legitimate. We believe this person or thing deserves credit for who they are and what they do. In *respect* we listen to and seriously consider what the other person says or does. Although it isn't mandatory that we *appreciate* them, the two emotions generally go together. When we do these things with ourselves, we are practicing *self-respect*.

- **Responsibility:** *Responsibility* can be thought of both as an emotion and a way of behaving. It literally means "to answer back." To live the emotion of *responsibility* means we "answer for our actions," and it's similar to being *accountable*. There are certain emotions and their consequent behaviors that we assume all people know and know how to do. *Responsibility* is one of them, although from an ontological understanding of emotions, we would say that our capacity for it is learned and that it can even be thought of as a skill.

- **Reverence:** "To stand in awe of" and "to honor" are aspects of *reverence*. The story of something we *revere* is that it is of significance, provokes fear, and is larger than us. To *revere* nature or deities acknowledges the relationship we have with them. *Reverence*, like *awe*, shows us those things we believe are beyond the human scale and often of which we are a part.

■ **Righteousness:** When we believe we are right and we are the only one who is right, that belief generates the emotion of *righteousness.* As an emotion, it allows us to be completely sure of our beliefs. We need not question what we believe if we know it is the truth. On the other side, if we "know" we are right, then anyone with another view or belief must be wrong. It can also have a moral quality in that it equates "being wrong" with "being bad." It is easy to see how this emotion is at the root of many conflicts, particularly when both parties are committed to it. A similar but less extreme emotion is *certainty,* in which I'm sure I am correct, but it has less of a moral quality than *righteousness.*

■ **Sacrifice:** What do we see when someone is sacrificing themselves for another? Most often we simply see one person helping another or coming to their aid. That could describe many emotions—*care, service, compassion*—so how do we know when it is *sacrifice* and not something else? The key is to hear the story the helper has about the impact their actions have on themselves. What makes a *sacrifice* a *sacrifice* is that the act of helping another depletes us. In contrast to *service,* which energizes us, sacrifice reduces our energy and resilience. That does not make *sacrifice* in any way a "bad" emotion, but it does mean that if we live in sacrifice as a mood, it is not sustainable. *Sacrifice* is often seen as noble or heroic or a sign of love, which it can be, but that does not change its nature of unsustainability. If we take the extreme case of a parent saving their child from drowning and then drowning themselves, we have such an example. It was a choice freely made, and most of us would consider it a supreme act of love. It is also one that is not sustainable or, as we sometimes say, is the "ultimate sacrifice."

Many times people in situations where their role is to help others—parents, medical providers, social workers, teachers—find they are confused by why they are exhausted from doing work they deeply care about. It could be that the answer is in a lack of clearly understanding the distinction between *service* and *sacrifice*. The only significant difference ontologically is that the first nurtures us and the second drains us. Their outward appearance and even the way we think about those actions are largely the same, but the impact on us is different.

A story of the author's illustrates this (Dan): "When I was growing up, my mother was a teacher, my father a minister, and they had five children to care for. I observed my parents constantly helping others. When talking about their work, they only called it *service,* and I never heard the idea of *sacrifice* spoken about at home. So I grew up without any distinction between the two. When I saw *sacrifice,* I thought it was *service.* When I began working myself, I continued the pattern, and it wasn't until I reached exhaustion that I learned to distinguish between the two. Knowing that I had a choice and that both were valid emotions to act from made a tremendous difference in my self-care and in my mood. Previously I found myself in *resentment,* meaning I believed I had no choice but to do work that drained me. Learning that I could freely choose when I would *sacrifice* and when I would *serve* others profoundly changed the way I live my life."

■ **Sadness:** *Sadness* is an emotion that we generally do not welcome. When we experience it, we often try to distract ourselves, and our friends may try to distract us from it as well. If we took the interpretation that *sadness* is informing us that "I have lost something I care about," we would be able to see that *sadness* is essential to understand what is important to us. If I am sad because my car was in an accident, it is telling me that I have lost something I care about. Perhaps it is the beauty I appreciated before, or perhaps it is that I value the utility of having a car and have lost that at least temporarily. Or it could be that I will have to pay a deductible on my insurance, and I care about using that money for something else. If a friend I have coffee with each month moves to another city, I might be *sad* for the loss of the possibility of having coffee together. I have not lost my friend, nor have I lost the possibility of drinking coffee, but only of doing it in a way that was important to me. A great deal of *fear* is associated with *sadness* because of the belief that if we stay in it too long, it may develop into depression. Ontologically this is not generally a concern, as we understand depression to be closer to the emotion of *hopelessness*. This is an example of why having clear distinctions between emotions can be useful.

Satisfaction (and Dissatisfaction): If we think about the idea that every emotion is offering us information, we might ask what satisfaction is telling us. Literally *satis* means "enough" and *dis- + satis* would mean "not enough." Ontologically the two can be seen to be telling us what we believe we have enough of in life and what we believe we are lacking. So satisfaction isn't telling us that "we have all we want" or "all we would like to have," but that we "have enough." It is common for people to confuse dissatisfaction with whining or complaining, but they are different things altogether. *Dissatisfaction* means "I don't have enough" of something, *complaining* is only valid if connected to an unfulfilled promise, and *whining* is simply expressing that "I don't like the way life is."

So what purpose do *satisfaction* and *dissatisfaction* fulfill? On a basic level they tell us if we believe we have enough food or not, enough warmth or not, enough money or not. Beyond this, they have a connection with our purpose as human beings. People who feel *satisfied* in life are engaged in activities that allow them to share their gifts and talents. When people complain of being *dissatisfied* in their work, it is often because they do not have this opportunity. So *satisfaction* is a kind of emotional compass that points to our reason for being here.

- **Sensual/Sensuous:** Although these are different emotions, they have an intertwined history. *Sensual* comes from Latin, meaning "of the senses" or something we experience through our senses. Over time it came to have a less than pure connotation and began to include physical activities that were considered shameful. In other words, a growing connection with sexual activities emerged. *Sensuous* was coined in the 1640s by John Milton to try to recapture the original meaning of something we experience with the senses. Today we don't tend to distinguish them or even be aware of the difference. Both emotions allow us to put our attention and appreciation on the physical experiences of life.

- **Sentimental:** From Medieval Latin, meaning "feeling or affection." To be *sentimental* means to have a tender or affectionate approach and to think of the world and relationships in this way.

- **Service:** Although *service* originated with the Latin word for "slave," we have not carried that meaning forward. We understand *service* as "care for others." An important aspect is that in the act of *service,* we are nourished. This contrasts with *sacrifice*, wherein we are caring for others, but it depletes us or costs us in terms of energy. The confusion comes because the actions of the two are similar, and it is the story or outcome for us personally that makes the difference.

■ **Shame:** *Shame* is the emotion that takes care of our public identity. It arises when we are aware that we have broken the rules or standards of our community. Our predisposition is to hide from that community. It doesn't necessarily mean that what we have done is ethically or morally wrong, but it is wrong according to the community of which we are a part. This is particularly important to understand when considering organizations, cultures, or nations. If the standard within an organization or industry is that you "get all you can whether you need it or not, regardless of the consequences" (which describes the emotion of *greed*), then to act in this way in that community will not provoke shame. In fact, the opposite is true. If you do not behave *greedily* you would be behaving contrary to the norms and would probably feel shame or have others believe you should feel it. So shame has a strong role in maintaining the culture of a group and keeping behaviors aligned.

■ **Sincerity:** "Whole," "pure," and "unmixed" are a few of the descriptors from Latin. Ontologically to be *sincere* means that what you are thinking privately is the same as what you are saying publicly. You are transparent and do not have a hidden agenda. It is an essential emotion to master in terms of building *trust*. Because we can have emotions about our emotions, there are people who are *sincere* about being *sincere* but are unable to be *sincere*. *Sincerity*, like other emotions, can be learned and is strengthened through practice.

■ **Skepticism:** Like *cynicism,* this emotion has a Greek historical derivation associated with a philosopher. It comes from the Greek word *skeptikos,* plural *Skeptikoi* or "the Skeptics," who were followers of Pyrrho (the Greek philosopher who lived c.360–c.270 BCE). This meant that they were "inquiring and reflective." That is still our meaning, although we often understand the inquiry to be directed at finding fault or weakness in an argument. The emotion of *skepticism* is most useful in helping us distinguish those things we will believe from those things we won't. As such, it is an essential skill in understanding and decision-making. It can be thought of as an opposite of *naiveté.*

■ **Smugness:** To be *smug* means we are confident of our ability and we have the air of superiority. It has similarities with *arrogance,* but is generally subtler and lower in intensity.

■ **Stubborn:** The root of the word *stubborn* is not clear, although it is certainly not Latin. It means that I have a belief I'm unwilling to change. My predisposition will be to remain fixed in my place or my idea. *Stubbornness* serves us to take a stand for what we believe is right or to remain *loyal.* On the other hand, it can get in the way of learning or change and keep us in the dark. It has a relationship to *persistence,* but is about remaining where I am rather than continually pressing ahead.

■ **Surprise:** The Latin root means "to overtake," which is what happens to us when we experience it. Our awareness is overtaken by something we did not expect. The predisposition of *surprise* is to check our facts or understanding. Like certain other emotions, *surprise* is not necessarily positive or negative, but describes the experience of the world overtaking us in some way.

- **Suspicion:** *Suspicion* is the emotion that challenges our *trust*. It clues us in to the possibility that our trust is misplaced or needs to be reexamined. That is the predisposition of *suspicion*. Being *suspicious* does not mean the other person is wrong or that we are right in our idea, only that there is a doubt about our previous way of understanding that calls for us to investigate. Being *suspicious* does not give us the right to accuse the other person, but its message is that there may be questions worth asking.

- **Sympathy:** *Sympathy* is the emotion that allows us to understand the emotions of others because we have experienced something similar. It literally means a "fellow-feeling" or a "community feeling." In *sympathy* we can resonate with the emotion of the other person without "taking on" their emotion, which is what occurs in *empathy*. You might think of it as a half step away from the emotion of the other person. You can understand their experience but are not having the same experience. You are not disengaged but are not fused with them either. The value of *sympathy* is that we can be with another person and they can feel that we understand, but we can still maintain our emotional independence. This allows conversations that *empathy, pity,* or *compassion* do not.

- **Tenderness:** From the Latin for "soft or tender," this is the emotion from which we care for others. The story of *tenderness* is that "I am safe and will be treated gently in this person's presence and care." Because *tenderness* often has to do with physical treatment and because it promotes intimacy, it can be confused with *eroticism* or *sexuality*. As a consequence, when a culture has a fear of those two emotions, it may make *tenderness* suspect. The line between those emotions has to do with the story (or intention) of the person offering them. And those lines can become blurry and, at times, be crossed.

■ **Terror:** Literally "to be filled with *fear*." While *anxiety* is the belief that something may happen to harm me but the source of the danger isn't clear, *terror* is the belief that something may happen to harm me and the source of the danger could be anywhere. In other words, no place is safe. Its value to anarchists or what we now call terrorists is obvious. In *terror* we are inclined to stop activities that engage us in the world, such as social gatherings, celebrations, and travel in order to feel greater safety.

■ **Thankful:** To be *thankful* is to acknowledge an exchange of value. When we give *thanks* by saying a blessing at the dinner table, we are acknowledging that we have received something of value and are expressing our appreciation. If I thank my mechanic for fixing my car, I'm saying that what he did for me and what I did for him are a satisfactory exchange. *Thankfulness* is different than *gratitude,* which is the acknowledgment of a gift. Thankfulness means we believe we have received something of value equal to what we have given.

■ **Timid:** When we are fearful of life in general, we can be thought of as *timid*. It is the story that many or most things have some danger and it is better to avoid them. Of course, our predisposition is to hide or to make ourselves scarce. The value of *timidity* is that if we do live in a situation that is dangerous to us or we are weak and unable to face the challenges of life, it keeps us safe. It should not be confused with *shyness*, which is the inclination to avoid being seen. *Shyness* is not necessarily provoked by fear but more by a desire for invisibility.

■ **Tolerance:** When we are being *tolerant*, our thought is that we don't agree with the other person, but "we will go along with them until they realize we are right." We sometimes talk about the emotions of *tolerance* and *acceptance* interchangeably, but they are very different. Whereas *acceptance* is acknowledging what is and not needing to change it, *tolerance* is when we want the person to change and are playing a waiting game until they do. Both have to do with our capacity to get along with others, but *tolerance* is a much lower bar. It literally means "to endure" or "to bear."

■ **Triviality:** *Triviality* comes from the Latin *trivialis*, meaning "common, commonplace, or vulgar." When we *trivialize* something, we take away its importance and beauty. We are unable to give it serious consideration. *Trivializing* is a way to avoid something important that we do not want to face. In that sense it is similar to *denial*, but it is active. It can have value when we use it to dismiss the importance of something to allow us to carry on, but it can get in the way of learning and relationships. Our predisposition in *triviality* is to ridicule or make fun of others and their ideas.

■ **Trust:** Ontologically trust is the emotion that allows us to coordinate action with others. We have traditionally understood trust from a "moral" perspective, meaning it had to do with our "goodness" or "badness" as human beings. While you're free to use this interpretation,

111

it is more useful to think of *trust* as a "risk assessment tool" based on *sincerity, competence,* and *reliability.* When we believe there is not excessive risk based on these dimensions of the other person, we will interact with them. If, according to our standard, we feel there is excessive risk, we will not interact with them and we will explain it by saying we do not *trust* them.

Trust is not just about other people. We have a self-assessment of *trust* and we evaluate groups, systems, processes, and technologies in terms of trust. When sufficient *trust* exists, we are willing to interact with others. When we *distrust,* we are less willing or not willing at all. There is also the condition of low *trust,* when we do not have enough experience with someone to evaluate his or her sincerity, competence, and reliability. *Trust* is a skill and competence and thus can be learned, practiced, and improved.

Without *trust,* it would be impossible to have relationships, create organizations, make requests, or accept promises from other people. If we do not have a high enough level of *trust,* we will not board an airplane, buy a product, or accept a job. In fact, there are very few activities we can undertake in life that do not have a dimension of trust involved.

■ **Wonder:** When we experience the emotion of *wonder,* we are encountering something miraculous, marvelous, or astonishing, and it is often something we do not understand. If the experience is scary, it provokes *awe,* but if it is something we consider positive or beneficial, we experience *wonder.* Our predisposition will be to continue the experience. *Wonder* is one of the emotions that connect us with something bigger than ourselves. It takes us into a larger universe and helps us recognize that what we are experiencing is in some way extra-ordinary.

■ **Yearning:** *Yearning* informs us that we are separated from a person or thing of primary importance to us. It is telling us something about our deepest desires. It is often experienced as a hollowness or pain in the area of the heart, and is prompting us to do everything in our power to get closer. *Yearning* informs us not just what we care about but what we do not want to live without. It can be confused with *desire* or even *infatuation,* but is more profound than either. Perhaps "burning desire" comes closest to describing *yearning* poetically.

A new view of anxiety

The emotional learning that has most been useful has to do with anxiety and the distinctions I've learned between anxiety, fear, and doubt. I'd been living with a fair amount of anxiety around my health, and as a result my future. Anxiety can be defined ontologically as "the fear of some unknown threat(s)." What I learned from Dan is to reflect and see if I can shift the anxiety into fear or doubt. By shifting anxiety into fear of a specific threat, I'm able to take action to resolve or mitigate the threat. By transforming anxiety into doubt, I can see that this is something I've never done before, and therefore the doubt is not unwarranted. I can then call upon courage to proceed into this new territory. I now view anxiety as a beginning point rather than a place to wallow, a call for inquiry and reflection to identify exactly what is causing me concern.

—C.R.

Bringing emotions into my coaching

I am an executive coach and I was trained in a traditional way, using conversation as my primary tool. I didn't believe that I could introduce emotions into my coaching, particularly since it was done in a meeting room with glass walls, making the coachee visible to other employees. I wouldn't know what to do if my coachee got angry or started crying. What I began to learn through my emotions training with Dan and Lucy was that working with emotions is much more subtle than making someone cry.

I learned that being able to hear the specific emotions the coachee was expressing allowed me to step back with them in order to question their interpretation of events. Then together we could determine if their interpretation was true or something they just thought was true. In this way they were able to learn to shift emotions and to approach their problems in new ways. For me it was a great addition to the methods and tools I already had. It allowed me to coach in a much more effective way, and according to my coachees helped them learn about themselves emotionally. As a side note, I now have coachees asking me to work with them in the area of emotional learning because they have become aware through a 360-degree evaluation or other interaction that it is an area of weakness for them. In this area, even little steps make a big difference.

—M.O.

Chapter 4

EMOTIONAL CLUSTERS

Some emotions have similarities that can make them easy to confuse or difficult to distinguish clearly. The authors call these *emotional clusters,* and they could be thought of like clusters of grapes. These emotions are distinct, but it isn't unusual to find them together. Because they sometimes feel similar, the way to distinguish one from another is through their story or the information they are trying to give us. Other times the distinction can be found in their differing predispositions.

In this section we will briefly describe how these emotions relate to each other, but these are the basis for much deeper work with clients when we use them in coaching. A single set of distinctions can sometimes be the basis of several coaching sessions when the coachee or learner understands them and begins to apply them to their own life.

The following are clusters we find to be common in our work:

- **Joy and Excitement:** The primary difference between these two emotions has to do with the energy level and its sustainability. Joy can be thought of as "a profound sense of well-being," while excitement is "activity with elevated energy." They are both thought of as "good" emotions and ones we pursue, although in modern times we tend to choose *excitement* over *joy*. Ontologically *joy* is sustainable indefinitely, while *excitement* needs higher and higher levels of energy in order to be sustained. This can be seen in the emergence of extreme sports as a societal example. *Joy* tends to be a more common emotion in introverts, while *excitement* tends to be common in extroverts. This makes sense given that introverts seek satisfaction in experiences that produce inner meaning while extroverts find satisfaction in external stimulation. Given this, it isn't uncommon for introverts to be yearning for a little more *excitement* and extroverts trying to understand how they can experience more *joy*.

■ **Tenderness, Eroticism, and Passion:** These three are often confused when they are connected with sexuality. Tenderness is the desire to create safety, eroticism to "become one" with, and passion to be intensely connected with another. Of the three, eroticism comes closest to suggesting sex, since it is the desire to meld with another. However, if we want to understand the emotion fully, we need to consider that eroticism is also what has people commit to meditation or commune with nature, and it can be the emotion that allows immersion in artistic endeavors; its core is the desire "to become one with another." Tenderness shows up when a child comes to us after a fall, and without thinking, we open our arms to embrace them. That very act is one of producing a safe space for them in a world that, to them, suddenly appears unsafe. Passion literally means "to suffer" or to have a yearning desire to be close. Passion can be religious, artistic, romantic, or erotic. Being able to see these three in their fullest expression allows them to be a rich source of engagement in life.

■ **Anxiety, Fear, and Doubt:** These three emotions feel quite similar in the body and thus are often confused. There is a somatic tightness, shallow breath, and hesitation in all three, but where they differ is in their stories. Anxiety means "something may happen to injure me, but I'm not sure of the source," fear means "something may happen to injure me, and I am sure of the source," and doubt means "I'm unsure about succeeding because I've never done this before."

When we need to make a presentation to a group of a hundred people, which of these emotions is it that challenges us? If we've never made a presentation to that large a group or on that topic, perhaps it is *doubt*. If we've had the experience of being ridiculed in the past when speaking publicly, perhaps it is *fear*. If we simply have an uneasy feeling that produces the circular thinking, we call the worry we are experiencing *anxiety*. None of these feel particularly good to most people, so why bother trying to understand and not avoid them? The problem with trying to simply dismiss them is that they are a part of us, so there is no getting rid of them. However, if we can understand what they are trying to communicate, we can navigate them and even turn them into support.

Doubt is telling me "I'm in new territory, so don't assume I know or that I am prepared." If we think back to the example of the presentation, once I listen to doubt's message and acknowledge that this is indeed new territory and I have "turned over all the rocks," I can thank doubt for its support and put my attention on the experience I want to create for my listeners. *Fear* is alerting me to a specific thing that could happen or I believe could happen because of some past experience. A way to distinguish the two is to ask questions such as, "Is the situation the same? Am I the same? It is truly a possibility that 'that thing' will happen here? What could I do to be sure it doesn't? How prepared can

I be?" *Anxiety* is telling me to consider that there are things I cannot identify that could derail me. Is there someone I could ask what I might be missing in my preparation? How could I get a look at what I might be blind to? Each of these emotions exists for its own reason and is, in its own way, trying to help me or take care of me. The reason emotions such as these are uncomfortable is to get my attention. If they felt good or even neutral, I would not pay attention to them the way I do when they make me uncomfortable. The discomfort has a purpose, and that purpose ultimately has to do with supporting me.

■ **Courage and Boldness:** *Courage* is the ability to act in the presence of *fear, boldness* is stepping into action when we perceive danger. In a sense we could think of *courage* as the emotion we need when we face fear and need to respond to it, and *boldness* as the emotion that lets us move ahead freely in situations that may hold danger. The root of each gives us an insight into the distinction. *Courage* comes from the French word for "heart," while *boldness* come from the Anglo-Saxon word for "strength" or "confidence."

■ **Service and Sacrifice:** Service and sacrifice are both focused on the care of others. One of the challenges in distinguishing them is that they look very much the same in action. The key difference ontologically is the impact on the person giving the care. A useful interpretation is that we are in *service* when we do something for others and it *nourishes* us. It may still be tiring, but it fills us and renews our energy. *Sacrifice* is when we do something for others and it depletes us. We may still choose to do it, but the care cannot be sustained indefinitely.

An extreme example of *sacrifice* is when someone gives up his or her own life to save another; for instance, in a fire or wartime. We even call this the supreme *sacrifice*. What is occurring is that the person making the *sacrifice* is extending care to the other in a way that is not sustainable. The difference then has to do with sustainability. It is sometimes a mystery to people engaged in work they love that involves the care of others that they find themselves exhausted and even resentful. Why would that happen when they are doing something they choose and believe to be a good thing? The answer is that they do not see this distinction. In fact, they probably call the *sacrificing* they are doing *service*. This is common among parents, teachers, doctors, and social workers. Because we have not learned the distinction between *service* and *sacrifice*, we cannot see the difference and thus do not have a choice.

■ **Pride and Arrogance:** *Pride* is an emotion many people are conflicted about. On the one hand, we want to be proud of our children or work we have done, but we also believe that "pride goes before a fall" and should be avoided. Part of this confusion may be that we are talking about two different emotions without realizing it. Ontologically *pride* means believing "I am or have done something worthwhile and want to tell others about it." Arrogance is believing I am or have done something good and wanting to let others know, but it includes the belief that this makes me better than others. So *arrogance* carries an additional element.

Pride, unlike arrogance, is not an emotion that has to do with positioning ourselves relative to others, but is only expressing a belief in our own goodness. There has been a traditional interpretation in both Protestantism and Catholicism of pride as an emotion we should avoid, as it is sinful. The word "pride" was the translation given to a fourth-century Greek text that is today our word "boasting" and thus would be closer to our word *arrogance*. Given this strong historical interpretation and the lack of distinction

119

between pride and arrogance, many people get stuck without an emotion that allows them to share what they believe is good about themselves. A reinterpretation of these two emotions can provide that.

■ **Guilt and Shame:** *Guilt* and *shame* are emotions that we try to avoid because of their unpleasant feeling. If we can accept this unpleasantness as their way of getting our attention, we may find that *guilt* tells us when we have transgressed our personal values while *shame* does the same for the values of our community. The important message we miss when we simply wallow in "feeling bad" is the good news that we do have strong values and it is clear what they are. *Guilt* and *shame* show us that we are aware of our values or those of our community and when we believe we have broken them.

Guilt and *shame* are good examples of emotions about which we have emotions. We don't share our emotion of *guilt* because we believe it is against the rules of the community, and thus feel *shame*. This pattern of one emotion overshadowing another is important to learn about, because our primary emotion can be masked by a second and we fail to see its message. For instance, if we experience an injustice, our reaction would be the emotion of *anger,* but if we feel *embarrassed* that we are *angry,* we will be acting from the *embarrassment* and miss what the *anger* is trying to tell us.

■ **Compliance and Commitment:** *Compliance* and *commitment* are two often-confused emotions. *Compliance* means "I will do it because I don't believe I have a choice." *Commitment* means "I will put my full resources into it getting done because I choose to." This is a very important distinction, particularly in regard to promises. It may be that *compliance* to fulfill a request is sufficient—for instance, when we ask the waiter to bring us salt—but in more important or difficult situations we will be better served if the performer *commits*. The highest *commitment* is when the performer cares about the promise being fulfilled as much as the requester. And it is important to remember that even a promise made in full and complete *commitment* does not guarantee completion or success. Commitment, besides being an emotion, is also a skill. Generally we assume that everyone knows how to "be committed," but in fact it is something we have learned. When we cannot see commitment as both an emotion and a skill, it is a vague and difficult aspect of life to teach.

Indignance and Anger: These are two more emotions we often confuse. *Anger* is, of course, very familiar to most of us, but *indignance* we tend to know less about. *Anger* is one of the emotions we most strongly try to control because we tend to see it as one of the most dangerous. It shows up when we experience something we believe is unjust, and our predisposition is to punish the source of the injustice. A child hitting his or her father for refusing to buy an ice cream cone is doing just that. One partner giving the silent treatment to the other may be doing so as a punishment for what they perceive is unjust. Although we can be angry with ourselves, often *anger* is an outwardly directed energy. It is about "them," but when it is about us, we will punish ourselves. *Dignity* is the emotion generated when we believe "I am a legitimate human being with the rights and responsibilities of every other human being." *Indignance* is the emotion that allows us to recognize violation of our boundaries and to defend them. In *indignance* there is no desire to punish another person, but only to take care of ourselves.

Neither emotion requires grand gestures or drama, although we often see *anger* in particular expressed this way. This is the distinction between an

121

emotion (an energy co-created by our story) and drama (the level of energy and manner in which we express an emotion). *Anger* can be lived very quietly—"smoldering" is the adjective sometimes used to describe this—or it can be loud and animated. *Indignance* actually calls for us to restrain and defend ourselves in a way that is *dignified*. We should not believe that a dramatic display of either emotion is evidence of its depth. When we do not have a distinction between these two emotions we may "throw the baby out with the bathwater" in relation to *dignity*. If we believe *anger* is dangerous or bad and avoid it, we may lose access to *indignance* in order to protect ourselves. This is a common breakdown for people who have grown up in an environment in which *anger* was taboo.

■ **Compassion, Empathy, Sympathy, and Pity:** These four emotions are regularly used interchangeably or are seen as the same thing, but they are not. *Empathy* is the capability to share or match the emotion of the other person, *sympathy* is to resonate or recall from experience the same emotion as the other is experiencing, *compassion* is to be present with the other person without adopting or judging their emotion, and *pity* is to be aware of the other's emotions or needs and to believe they need our help because in some way we are superior. They have different applications in relationships. *Empathy* serves us when a friend is in deep sadness and we simply want to be connected with them emotionally. *Sympathy* allows us to understand the emotion of the other person, which can help us determine what actions might be appropriate, such as sending a card or acknowledgment of some kind. *Compassion* allows us to legitimize another's emotion without "falling into it" or "taking it on" and is thus extremely useful in coaching or leadership. *Pity* signals us that others need our help—for instance, when we see a dog hit by a car, and we realize that without our superior knowledge of what to do for them, they will suffer or perhaps die. *Pity* and *compassion* in particular can also be experienced toward ourselves. *Self-pity* is believing that I cannot go on without the support or attention of another person, and *self-compassion* means being with my emotions without judgment or trying to change them. In this case, *self-compassion* and *self-acceptance* are very close.

Each of the four also has limits. *Empathy* may not be available to us in all situations. It probably is not possible for a man to truly *empathize* with a mother whose child has died. As a parent, he could feel *sympathy* if he has experienced a similar loss, but since he has not had the experience of gestating and giving birth to a child, true *empathy* would not be available. This does make him less understanding, but only means he has different emotions available. In some cases we are unable to feel *sympathy* because we do not have a similar experience to relate to. For instance, if every night of my life I have had a home to go to, I might not have the ability to *sympathize* with someone who is homeless. I could feel *compassion, care, concern,* or *pity,* but not *sympathy. Compassion* requires that I am able to maintain my own emotional center while at the same time accepting and acknowledging the other person's emotion. That is a skill not everyone has developed.

Anger, Frustration, and Resentment: *Anger* informs us that something we are experiencing is, in our view, unjust. *Frustration* is the story that "it should have already happened." *Resentment* is the belief that "it shouldn't be this way" or "I shouldn't have to do this." *Anger* predisposes us to punish, *frustration* to look for ways to move ahead, and *resentment* to get even or take revenge. The first step in navigating any of these emotions is to remove the moral interpretation and to normalize them as emotions. Once we do that, we can remove our prejudgment and simply see them as emotions. If what we are experiencing is *anger*, then the effective response will be to design actions that correct the injustice we perceive. If it is *frustration*, the question may be what standard we are using for our assessment that things "should" be moving faster. Understanding that our standard may be ungrounded or naïve can sometimes bring *acceptance*. Another path is to look for how things could be speeded up. Resolving *resentment* can also take the path of *acceptance* that what is done is done. Or it can take the path of questioning the assessment with "shouldn't." Why "shouldn't" it be this way? Generally, the answer is simply that it isn't what we expected rather than it being right or wrong.

■ **Sadness, Regret, and Disappointment:** *Sadness* is the loss of something we care about so, far from being "in the way" as an emotion, it points directly to our cares. It is valuable to think of sadness as "losing access" to something we care about, because sometimes we dismiss the importance of changes where we cannot identify a "thing" we have lost. An example is that if a friend I enjoy spending time with moves to a distant city, I may feel *sad* not because I've lost my friend but because I can no longer enjoy our times together as we did. So the loss is of the possibility of being with the other person. This is the type of thing many of us will shrug off and diminish, when it can be the cause of the *sadness*.

Regret means that I wish I had made different choices in the past because I believe that if I had, my life would be better. That story presupposes that "life would have been better if…," but this is something we cannot know. It could be true, but life could also have turned out worse. If we accept those points, we can sometimes release the *regret*. An interesting point is that we sometimes say we should have made a different decision, but upon examination, we can see that given who we were at that moment, we could not have made a different decision, so our regret is groundless. We believe we could have made a different decision because the decision we made brought us the awareness we have now, so the logic does not hold up.

"Appoint" comes from Old French, to "make ready or arrange," and, of course, *dis* means "did not." Ontologically, disappointment means that life as we are experiencing it and life as we expected it do not align. Life is not happening as we thought it would. This occurs because we are continually creating a story of what the future will be like. Our version of *how life will be* comes from two places. One is when others make promises to us and the other is a fabrication based on the possibilities we can imagine. These possibilities come from our experience and history and also from the experience and history of others. When a promise is not fulfilled or the experience isn't as we expected, the emotion that shows up is *disappointment*. The message many people take from disappointment is that "something is wrong," but ontologically it means that "life isn't happening as I thought it would." If the expectation came from a promise that was not fulfilled, my recourse is to lodge a complaint with the promisor. However, if my expectation came from my own imagination, then I must take responsibility for its creation and realize that it is not reality that is wrong but it is my story that is out of alignment with life.

Liking and Loving: Ontologically, *liking* someone means that we enjoy being in their company and would like to continue or renew it. We may enjoy it because it is fun or exciting or even challenging, but there is something in the interactions that we enjoy. *Love* has many, many interpretations, but the one that seems most appropriate ontologically is that "*love* is the ability to accept someone as they are and hold them as a legitimate human being." It could be thought of as a combination of *acceptance, dignity,* and *respect,* in which *acceptance* means that we acknowledge the other person "is as they are," *dignity* means we believe the other person is "enough just as they are," and *respect* means "we value the other person just as they are." You can see that *loving* someone does not imply that we enjoy being with them, but that we can respect and honor them as a human equal to ourselves and deserving of our respect. With this understanding, it is possible to love any person, even when we may not like them or enjoy being in their company. We can have a relationship that includes one, the other, both, or neither.

■ **Trust and Liking:** Many times leaders will say that they need to get people on their team to like each other so they can work together. To this end they organize picnics or other events to encourage employees to like each other. Interestingly, it turns out that *trust* has nothing to do with *liking* another person, and therefore we can have one without the other. *Liking* someone means enjoying being with him or her. *Trusting* someone means that we are willing to interact with them. If we take the example of a taxi driver, we can see that we need to trust him or her to get to the airport—*trust* meaning we believe he or she is sincere, competent, and reliable—but we do not need to like them. Since it is unlikely we have ever met them before, *liking* them is not an emotional possibility. If we do know them and also *like* them, it is lovely, but it is not necessary for hiring them to take us to the airport. We sometimes have friends whom we *like* but we do not necessarily *trust,* for instance, to be on time. We still enjoy being with them, but we also know they are not reliable in the domain of time.

126

The distinction between liking and trusting is important in all relationships, and it is helpful to think about which emotion serves us best in specific relationships and circumstances. It is important to *trust* and be *trusted* by our boss, but often people put more attention on *liking* or being *liked* by their boss in the mistaken belief that it will make working (coordinating action) with him or her easier. It is true that a boss might compensate on the basis of *liking* you, in which case it may be important to you to develop. In your relationship with your son or daughter, is it more important that there is *trust* or *liking*? Sometimes we go for *liking* because we see it as a form of *love* (which we talked about above), but that alone will not build *trust,* and *trust* is what we need in order to interact with confidence.

■ **Ambition and Enthusiasm:** The energy of *ambition* and *enthusiasm* can look very similar somatically and can even sound similar, and can thus be confused. *Ambition* means I will take actions to gain something for myself. *Enthusiasm,* from the Greek *en theos,* means "connected to the gods." As an emotion, *ambition* is much more about me or us as human beings, whereas *enthusiasm* is commitment to a cause greater than myself or ourselves. This makes a difference in terms of sustaining energy and maintaining focus. *Ambition* can sometimes burn out, since the energy is coming from our humanness. We can become consumed with our *ambition* and lose sight of any higher cause or purpose which *enthusiasm* provides.

■ **Wonder and Awe:** *Wonder* and *awe* are emotions most of us have lost touch with as adults. Children seem to experience *wonder* as a natural part of their interactions with a world they do not know. *Awe* we only know as part of the slang "awesome," which has little to do with *awe* as an emotion.

127

Both show up when we encounter something powerful and unknown. Both relate to the recognition of things beyond our day-to-day experience and understanding, although *wonder* lacks the terror or fear that *awe* includes. We tend to move toward something we find *wonder-ful,* but to back away from an event that produces *awe* due to the element of fear.

In a 2015 study, Dacher Keltner, a professor of psychology at Berkeley, published an article on a research study that showed experiencing awe several times each week had "a pronounced impact on markers related to inflammation," and thus contributed to physical health. It is difficult to say whether what Keltner was studying was *wonder* according to our interpretation, but his study does draw a link between emotions and health that we often forget.[1]

Beyond possible physical health benefits, connecting with *wonder* and *awe* can shift us out of emotions such as *boredom* and *ennui,* where we end up when we believe we understand everything in the universe around us and have become jaded.

■ **Jealousy and Envy:** Here are two more emotions that are related, confused, and have strong stories associated with them. *Jealousy* and *envy* fall into what we have considered the "bad emotions" category, and so we are uncomfortable acknowledging them even to ourselves. *Jealousy* means "I have a fear I will lose something or someone I care about." *Envy* means "there is something you have that I want in my life." Deep envy might include that I think I deserve it more than

---

1   Gretchen Reynolds, "An Upbeat Emotion That's Surprisingly Good for You," *New York Times Magazine,* March 29, 2015, http://mobile.nytimes.com/blogs/well/2015/03/26/an-upbeat-emotion-thats-surprisingly-good-for-you/?

you and want to take it from you, although this begins to move into *revenge.* Like *guilt* and *shame,* these two have messages for us that we often overlook. If I am *envious* of something you are or have, the message is that I would like that in my life. When I say that something is the "object of my desire," I am expressing *envy.* If I listen to the message of *envy,* I can either wallow in this desire or I can begin to strategize how to create something similar for myself. In reality, whatever you are or have won't fit into my life, so simply taking it from you won't resolve the *envy,* even though that is often what I believe. *Jealousy,* on the other hand, is telling me to "consider whether I really own whatever it is I fear losing, and to consider how to create a stronger bond other than ownership" (such as in relationships). It is trying to tell me that something or someone is of deep importance to me and to not overlook that fact. Often we misspeak by saying that we are "jealous of" another person, when in reality we are experiencing *fear* that someone else will be seen as more attractive than we are and thus we will lose the person we care about.

■ **Acceptance, Indifference, Ambivalence, and Resignation:** If there was an award for "most misunderstood" emotion, we would vote for *acceptance.* First of all, we confuse *acceptance* with acquiescence or surrender. Secondly, we see it as a passive emotion, when it can move us powerfully from one emotion or mood to another. *Acceptance* means "I acknowledge it is as it is." I am not agreeing with how it is. I am not resisting how it is. I am not endorsing how it is. I'm simply saying I understand that it is as it is. Between the emotions of *resignation* and *ambition* stands acceptance. We cannot move from one to the other without going through *acceptance.* *Acceptance* is the "you are here" marker on the map of emotions. Regarding it being passive, it is true that there are no actions associated with it, but we mistakenly think we need to "wait for *acceptance* to show up" when we are fully capable of declaring *acceptance* for a situation we no longer want to put our energy into.

Indifference means "one choice has no more appeal than another to me." *Ambivalence* means "I could be supportive if we go this way or if we go that way" and means that "the wind blows both directions." *Resignation* means that "I believe nothing I do will make any difference, so I will not put any energy into trying." Of the three, *resignation* is the one most often confused with *acceptance,* since neither has any physical actions associated with it except stillness. Linguistically they can even sound the same. When someone says "whatever," he or she could be in *acceptance* or *resignation* or even *indifference* or *ambivalence.* The only way of distinguishing is to investigate the deeper story of the speaker.

■ **Humility and Obsequiousness:** *Humility* literally means "of the earth" or "well grounded," although many people hear it as meaning "lowly" or "like dirt." *Humility* ontologically means "claiming only what is true about oneself," or in other words, "being real" or "being grounded." It has nothing to do with putting oneself below others as *obsequiousness* does. It is not a comparison with others. In *humility* I claim all that I am and claim nothing that I am not. I don't pretend to be "more than" or "less than." So a *humble* person does not deny the compliments others pay, but understands them as the assessments and views of that person. There is a long history of *humility,* meaning "to consider myself inferior to others," which is actually the definition for *obsequiousness.*

The interpretation that being *humble* makes me less important than other people has a tremendous impact on self-image and self-respect. Shifting our understanding of what *humility* is as an emotion and what it feels like can be tremendously liberating and can produce the belief that "I am what I am and that is enough."

Standing taller with dignity

During the Emotions Workshop in September 2015, I noticed my reflection in the mirror and that my body resembled the shape of a "?"—curved, concave chest from the base of the spine; taking short, shallow breaths; shoulders pulled toward each other, protecting my heart. Slumped over like a flower in the rain. As I listened to the definition of dignity on that specific day, in that precise moment my body shifted. Over time and with attention, I've transformed to an upright posture, shedding pain as a way of living; reclaiming my tall childhood stance. Same flower, now basking in the sun. I began to really believe that I am worthy, with or without pain. I stood taller, I could breathe with more ease, I had less pain. And knowing that I was enough, that I do belong, that I am safe—this is what living into my aliveness feels like. Naming dignity brought it to life. My heart was broken open, discovering so much room! I decided that I am enough, which allowed me to find my voice and to speak more clearly. I decide.

—R.L.

The Unopened Gift

Chapter 5

NOT QUITE EMOTIONS

A sk yourself, "How do I differentiate what is and isn't an emotion?" Do you have a clear answer? As important as emotions are in our makeup as human beings, it turns out that there is not a definitive list. This is likely a result of our lack of attention to the emotional domain's importance or our dismissal of it. Emotions have not been defined universally. There are some emotions we would all agree on, but there are many that are not clear-cut. In the authors' work trying to give precise interpretations to emotions, we have encountered expressions that are often thought of as emotions but don't pass the ontological test of giving us information, fueling our actions, and taking care of our human concerns. When they do not make the cut, we call them *conditions.* For us a condition is an emotional indicator, but not an emotion in the sense that it lacks one or more of the ontological criteria.

To be clear, we are not devaluing conditions or saying they are not as important as emotions, only that we cannot reconstruct them in the same way, so will not be able to navigate or work with them as we have suggested. They are certainly valid human experiences, but they fall into another category.

One example is when someone uses a somatic experience and calls it an emotion. A primary example is the use of the word "feelings." We often use this word interchangeably with "emotions," but "feelings" have traditionally pertained to the physical senses and have only recently been substituted for the word "emotions." The word "feeling" is used so broadly and vaguely that it is not a very precise way of talking about emotions. Another type of condition can be understood ontologically as an assessment. When we use "dismissed," "rejected," or "misunderstood," thinking they are emotions, we are actually sharing our assessment of the behavior of another person or group, and are not speaking precisely of an emotion. Other times we use a compact metaphor to describe an emotion without realizing it. "Overwhelm" is a very common example. "Overwhelm" is a literal description of the experience sailors went through when a large wave inundated and rolled over their ship, putting their lives in danger. It describes the sensation one might have in that situation, but is not accurately or simply an emotion.

The importance of distinguishing whether something is a true emotion or not has to do with our ability to navigate it. If we say we feel "hurt" by someone's actions, there is not an easy way to understand what to do about it or even what it means. Yes, we feel emotional discomfort or pain, but without identifying if the emotion generating that sensation is *indignance, disappointment, distrust,* or *disrespect,* we cannot design an effective path forward.

Here is a list of some of the most common conditions used in place of emotions, and there are many more. You will notice that the best the table can do is suggest which emotion or emotions are indicated by the listed condition, and thus its meaning is unclear without more investigation.

Condition	Root	Nature	Emotions Indicated
Abandoned	Late 14c. "to give up, surrender (oneself or something), give over utterly; to yield (oneself) utterly (to religion, fornication, etc.)," from Old French *abandoner* (12c.)	An **assessment** of how others are or have treated us	*Disloyalty* if by someone who is part of our community. *Disappointment* if one had the expectation of being included or taken care of.
Attacked	From Florentine Italian *attaccare (battaglia)* "join (battle)"	An **interpretation** of others' actions that cross our personal boundary and threaten us	*Indignance* for crossing my boundaries; *anger* if the attack is punishment; *resentment* or *vengeance* if the attack is to get even
Blame	Late Latin *blasphemare*, "revile, reproach"	Blame can be thought of as a **predisposition** for anger. It is a way in which we punish someone whom we believe has done something unjust	A predisposition to *anger*. Can also be related to *accountability* and is a mechanism to "call others to account."

Condition	Root	Nature	Emotions Indicated
Blue	As a music form, possibly c. 1895 (though officially 1912, in W.C. Handy's "Memphis Blues"); meaning "depression, low spirits" goes back to 1741, from adjectival *blue* "low-spirited," late 14c.	A **metaphor** calling the energy of the music my energy	*Sadness, depression, despondence,* or *resignation*
Centered	1590s, "to concentrate at a center," from *center*. Related: *centering,* meaning "to rest as at a center," is from 1620s.	A **state of being** at rest in the body, mind, and/or emotions	*Peace, serenity,* or *acceptance*
Comfort	Mid-14c., Anglo-French from *conforter* "to comfort." Meaning "offering physical comfort" is attested from 1769; that of "in a state of tranquil enjoyment" is from 1770.	A **physical state of being** in which there is an absence of stress	*Contentment, satisfaction,* or *complacence*

Condition	Root	Nature	Emotions Indicated
Connected	From Latin *connexionem,* "a binding or joining together," from *connexare,* "to fasten together, to tie, join together," from *com-* "together" + *nectere* "to bind, tie."	An **interpretation or assessment** of relative closeness with another	*Love, acceptance,* or *desire*
Control or controlling	From Latin *contra-* "against" + *rotulus,* diminutive of *rota* "wheel."	An **assessment** of my ability to maintain or change the direction of events in life	*Fear, anxiety,* or *jealousy*
Defensive	Directly from Latin *defendere* "ward off, protect, guard, allege in defense," from *de-* "from, away" + *fendere* "to strike, push."	A **physical action** to block another	*Indignance, fear,* or *resentment*
Degraded	From Old French *degrader* (12c.) "degrade, deprive (of office, rank, etc.)," from *des-* "down" + Latin *gradus* "step."	An **assessment** another is attempting to lower my sense of dignity	*Dignity, disrespect,* or *indignance*

Condition	Root	Nature	Emotions Indicated
Detached	From Old French *destachier*, from *des-* "apart" + *attachier*. "attach" from Old French *atachier* (11c.), earlier *estachier* "to attach, fix; stake up, support."	The **assessment** of not being part of something	*Despondence, sadness*, or *resignation*
Discounted	From Medieval Latin *discomputare*, from *dis-* "not" + *computare* "to count."	An **assessment** that we are not being considered or are not seen as important	*Disrespect* or *indignance*
Dismissed	Early 15c., from Latin *dimissus*, "send away, send different ways; break up, discharge; renounce, abandon," from *dis-* "apart, away" + *mittere* "send, let go."	An **assessment** that we are being sent away or intentionally set apart from what is important.	*Disrespect* or *indignance*

Condition	Root	Nature	Emotions Indicated
Distant	From Latin *distantem*, present participle of *distare* "to stand apart, be remote."	The **assessment** that we are not close to someone or something physically or emotionally	*Loneliness*
Drained	From Proto-Germanic *dreug-*, source of *drought*, *dry*, giving the English word originally a sense of "make dry."	**Physical** lack of energy or resources to initiate	*Sadness, resignation, resentment, despondence, despair*
Drama	From Late Latin *drama* "play, drama," from Greek *drama* (genitive *dramatos*) "play, action, deed," from *dran* "to do, act, perform."	To **physically amplify** the level of expression of an emotion—for instance, urgency—to get attention	Could be almost any, but *fear, irritation, enthusiasm, anger, passion* are common
Edgy	From *edge* + -*y*. Meaning "tense and irritable" is attested by 1837, perhaps from notion of being *on the edge*, at the point of doing something irrational.	**A physical sensation** of approaching a boundary I believe I shouldn't cross	*Frustration, impatience, anger, ire*

Condition	Root	Nature	Emotions Indicated
Emotional	From Latin *emovere* "move out, remove, agitate," from assimilated form of *ex-* "out"+ *movere* "to move." Meaning "characterized by or subject to emotions" is attested by 1857.	**A physical sensation** that my energy is changing and affecting my actions or choices	Could be related to many emotions, but indicates I'm experiencing a heightened state of emotional energy
Energetic	From Greek *energetikos* "active," from *energein* "to work, be in action, act upon."	**The physical sensation** of energy to act	*Enthusiasm, ambition, excitement* could be choices, along with many others in a heightened state
Excite	From Latin *excitare* "rouse, call out, summon forth, produce."	**A physical sensation** of elevated energy	*Enthusiasm* or *ambition* could be choices, along with many others in a heightened state
Feeling	C. 1400, "pertaining to the physical senses, sensory."	Awareness of a **physical sensation**	Not emotion-specific, but gives us the information that lets us know which emotion(s) we are experiencing

Condition	Root	Nature	Emotions Indicated
Flat	From Old Norse *flatr* "flat," from Proto-Germanic *flata-* (cognates: Old Saxon *flat* "flat, shallow," Old High German *flaz* "flat, level"). Sense of "prosaic, dull" is from 1570s, on the notion of "featureless, lacking contrast."	**A physical sensation** of dullness and inability to distinguish between emotions	*Boredom, resignation, ambivalence*
Fun	Probably a variant of Middle English *fonnen* "befool." "Diversion, amusement, mirthful sport."	**An activity** that we find enjoyable or delightful	*Joy, delight, excitement*
Great	From Old English *great* "big, tall, thick, stout; coarse."	The **physical sensation** of bigness or strength or energy.	*Joy, delight, ambition, enthusiasm, hope*
Grief	From Latin *gravare* "make heavy; cause grief," from *gravis* "weighty."	A **somatic heaviness** or lack of physical energy that is the predisposition of *sadness* but could be named to try to explain other emotions	*Sadness, despondence, despair, anguish*

Condition	Root	Nature	Emotions Indicated
Gutted	"Remove the guts of" (fish, etc.), late 14c., from *gut*; figurative use "plunder the contents of" is by 1680s.	The **physical experience** of losing possibility or sureness of what I thought I knew	*Incredulity, despair, anguish*
Hungry	Old English *hungor* "unease or pain caused by lack of food, craving appetite, debility from lack of food."	A **somatic sensation** of emptiness and desire to be filled	*Dissatisfaction, yearning, desire, passion, eroticism*
Hurt	C. 1200, "a wound, an injury"; also "sorrow, lovesickness." Reflexive sense of "suffering, feeling pain" recorded by 1944.	**A physical pain** that indicates something out of alignment or abnormal happening	*Anguish, sadness, remorse*
Icy	From Proto-Germanic *isa-* (cognates: Old Norse *iss*, Old Frisian *is*, Dutch *ijs*, German *Eis*), with no certain cognates beyond Germanic, though possible relatives are Avestan *aexa-* "frost, ice."	**An interpretation** of another's behavior toward us	*Resentment, jealousy, envy, disgust, anger*

Condition	Root	Nature	Emotions Indicated
Ignored	From Latin *ignorare* "not to know, disregard."	**Our interpretation** of another's behavior toward us	*Irritation, anger, disgust*
Macho	1928 (n.) "tough guy," from Spanish *macho* "male animal."	An **interpretation** of the actions of another	*Arrogance, pride*
Manic	From Late Latin *mania* "insanity, madness," from Greek *mania* "madness, frenzy; enthusiasm, inspired frenzy; mad passion, fury," related to *mainesthai* "to rage, go mad."	An **interpretation** of energy level being exceptionally high and chaotic	*Passion, confusion, elation, enthusiasm*
Negative	Directly from Latin *negativus,* "a prohibition; absence, nonexistence; opposite."	An **assessment** that something takes away from a good life	*Anger, frustration, irritation, resentment, cynicism, skepticism*

Condition	Root	Nature	Emotions Indicated
Organized	From Latin *organum* "instrument, organ."	An **interpretation** of the way one's life is ordered	*Prudent, peaceful*
Overwhelmed	Middle English from *over-* "above; highest; across; too much; above normal; outer," + *whelmen* "to turn upside down." Meaning "to submerge completely."	An **interpretation** that current conditions are not sustainable—they're bigger than we are	*Panic, fear, exhaustion, anxiety*
Positive	Directly from Latin *positivus* "settled by agreement."	An **interpretation** that good things are likely to happen	*Hope, trust*
Possibility	From Latin *possibilis* "that can be done," from *posse* "be able."	An **assessment** that there are things that could happen that haven't yet	*Hope, trust, ambition, enthusiasm*

Condition	Root	Nature	Emotions Indicated
Pragmatic	From Latin *pragmaticus* "skilled in business or law," from Greek *pragmatikos* "fit for business, active, business-like; systematic," from *pragma* "a deed, act; that which has been done; a thing, matter, affair," especially an important one.	**Interpretation** of a way in which someone is moving in life	*Caution, prudence*
Relief	Late 14c., "alleviation of distress, hunger, sickness, etc.; state of being relieved; that which mitigates or removes."	A **physical sensation** of reduced stress	*Trust, confusion (dissipating)*
Resistance	From Latin *resistere* "make a stand against, oppose."	A **physical sensation** of holding back or a mental holding out against beliefs counter to my own	*Fear, anxiety, caution, prudence*

Condition	Root	Nature	Emotions Indicated
Shock	"Violent encounter of armed forces or a pair of warriors," a military term, from Middle French *choc* "violent attack," from Old French *choquer* "strike against."	A **physical sensation** of being hit by something unexpected	*Surprise*
Short-Tempered	From Latin *temperare* "observe proper measure, be moderate, restrain oneself," also transitive, "mix correctly, mix in due proportion; regulate, rule, govern, manage."	A **rapid change** to an attacking emotion with little provocation	*Anger, irritation, frustration, aggravation, ire*
Stress	From Vulgar Latin *strictiare*, from Latin *stringere* "draw tight."	A **physical sensation** of tightness	*Anxiety, fear, exhaustion*
Tense	From Latin *tensus*, past participle of *tendere* "to stretch, extend."	A **physical sensation** of and inability to move due to tightness	*Anxiety, dread, fear, confusion*

Condition	Root	Nature	Emotions Indicated
Torn	"Act of ripping or rending," 1660s, from *tear*. Old English had *ter*, "tearing, laceration, thing torn."	A **physical sensation** or mental struggle	*Ambivalence, confusion*
Upbeat	"With a positive mood," 1947, apparently from *on the upbeat* "improving, getting better," attested from 1934 and a favorite of "Billboard" headline-writers in the early 1940s, from the musical noun *upbeat* (1869), referring to the beat of a bar at which the conductor's baton is in a raised position; from *up* (adv.) + *beat* (n.). The "optimistic" sense apparently for no other reason than that it sounds like a happy word (the musical upbeat is no more inherently "positive" than any other beat).	The **belief** that good things are going to happen to me	*Optimism, hope*

Condition	Root	Nature	Emotions Indicated
Vulnerable	From Latin *vulnerare* "to wound, hurt, injure, maim," from *vulnus* (genitive *vulneris*) "wound," perhaps related to *vellere* "pluck, to tear."	The **belief** that I will be injured by the words or actions of others and cannot defend myself	*Lack of dignity, self-respect, self-trust*
Weepy	Old English *wepan* "shed tears, cry; bewail, mourn over; complain."	The **physical sensation** that my body cannot contain my emotions and they will emerge as tears	*Anguish, sadness, fear*
Whiny	Old English *hwinan* "to whiz, hiss, or whistle through the air" (only of arrows), also *hwinsian* "to whine" (of dogs), ultimately of imitative origin (compare Old Norse *hvina* "to whiz," German *wiehern* "to neigh").	An **assessment** that life isn't the way I think it should be	*Discontent, dissatisfaction, entitlement, naiveté*

Discovering my conditions of satisfaction

My story begins in a situation that is probably very familiar to many people, regardless of culture, age, gender, etc. We were taught to succeed in life, whatever that means—to have decent income, have a nice family with kids, a house, a car . . . but nobody teaches you to listen to your gut to know what you want, how you want it, and if you want it. I am a lighting designer, and I always wanted to have my own studio. So I found a partner and we did very well very quickly. In fifteen years we went from two to twenty people, and from five to over sixty ongoing projects. I was trying to work as I did when we had fewer employees, where I was the one in charge of designing, acquiring the project, closing deals, handling public relations, being the organizer, and even the IT specialist.

But I noticed I had reached my limit when my stress went up to a level that had taken my sleep and was causing terrible consequences in my health and well-being. This affected my family, my friends, my colleagues, and my clients. I didn't know what to do (sound familiar?). My brother recommended that I work with Dan, an ontological coach, to find a new way of approaching my work. The sessions would be held via Skype in English, and English is not a language where I can express emotions as well as I can in Spanish or German. But I gave it a try.

I felt that things started to change in my life (I understand it does not change forever; it is an ongoing conscious work and process). We discussed establishing the conditions of satisfaction for my client, for me, and for all involved in the process of a project. I took the same conversation to my personal life, and this took a lot of burden and weight off my back. I was trying to satisfy everyone in the project and everyone in my personal life, and it was leaving me dissatisfied. And when I got desperate, I felt anger and deception. Establishing the conditions of satisfaction makes things easier for me. It gives me the chance to express my needs, my capabilities, and my limits, and listen to the real needs of the client—that in most cases are not as complex as I assumed. It is still a process of living the change, but considering what will produce satisfaction for me has been improving my personal relationships as well as the relationships with my clients.

—K.D.

Chapter 6

NAVIGATING EMOTIONS

Your Relationship with Moods and Emotions

It is common to hear people say that they want to "manage their emotions" or that they believe a certain person needs to have better "control over his or her emotions." These are concepts the authors do not adhere to, mostly because they are not effective. We believe we are better served by learning to navigate our emotions. There is little, if anything, we truly control in our lives, so why would we be able to control our emotions? We have choice about certain things, but that is different from control. We may want to control the world around us to shape it the way we would like, but eventually learn that for the most part we cannot. We do not control our thirst or hunger, our sleep, when we die, or even getting to work on time. We can be a big influence on these, we can make choices that affect them, and we can find clever ways to navigate them, but to say we control them, we believe, is to give ourselves too much credit.

The idea of *controlling* our emotions is a holdover from and closely connected to nineteenth-century science. As science grew as a way of understanding the world, its underlying beliefs entered our way of thinking about all areas of life. The fundamental idea that drove the development of scientific thought was that it allowed us to predict and control the world around us. That is the fundamental purpose of meteorology, for instance. The very essence of meteorology is that it allows us to predict if it will rain tomorrow so we can choose whether to take our umbrella when we go out, in order to control our comfort by not getting wet. In the longer term it allows us to predict, and at least try to control, what will happen in the coming seasons for agriculture or skiing. It can help us know if there will be dangerous waves on the lake or at the beach or if we should take steps to be sure our cold-sensitive crops do not freeze on a particular night. In other words, the science of meteorology exists to predict and control. We can apply this same concept to any science. Geology does the same for earth structure, to predict where we might find minerals, or for the prediction of earthquakes so that we can prepare or evacuate nearby residents. Western medicine applies the same principles to our health.

As this idea has been enormously successful in so many areas, we have assumed it applies to all areas of human life. However, when anyone has tried to apply the idea of control to emotions, we find that it is impotent. People will often say something like, "I don't want to remain angry but can't stop." In other words, they want to control the emotions they're experiencing, but find they are unable to. Control is a fantasy we create in order to feel safe.

Imagine kayaking down a stream. The effective relationship between you, your kayak, and the current is not one of control but of navigation. If you see you are approaching a rock in mid-stream, all that is necessary for you to avoid collision is to shift the direction of your kayak a bit to the left or right into a part of the current that will carry you past the outcrop. Navigation literally means *to drive or steer a ship*. In essence, this is the relationship available to us with emotions. Noticing them, understanding them, and choosing whether reaction or response will be more effective are all parts of navigating the current of emotions we are immersed in.

Shifting Emotions

When we find we are in or being affected by an emotion we don't want to be in, we often try to avoid it or to change it. Usually we try to do this through thinking. For instance, if we are sad, we might tell ourselves to "cheer up" or that we don't really have anything to be sad about. "It could be worse," we tell ourselves. And if we don't tell ourselves these things, our friends usually will. Most of us don't have much success with this technique, but we keep trying. Another, more useful, technique is to consider what emotion could serve us in place of the emotion we'd like to change. If we take fear as an example, we can try to talk ourselves out of fear, but generally the fear remains. If we understand that *courage* is the emotion that allows us to act in the presence of *fear*, then we could use that as a stepping-stone. We could put our attention on generating *courage* and put less attention on the *fear*. What will happen is that we will be able to move into action to take care of the task at hand. In the longer term, something else is happening, which is that we are building our capacity for *courage* and we are allowing the strength of *fear* to fade. In other words, we are not just acting but also learning in the emotional domain.

Another strategy for shifting emotions is not to try at all. If we take seriously the idea that "emotions come and emotions go," we realize that our emotional state is always shifting, whether we want it to or not. One possibility is embracing the emotion rather than trying to push it away. If we find ourselves in *sadness,* for instance, we could choose to "sit with it" and simply be *sad.* We are in essence saying that we believe *sadness* has work to do and we can allow it to do what it is here to do. In that quiet we could reflect on what the *sadness* is trying to tell us and on its purpose. If we know that *sadness* fundamentally means "I've lost something I care about," we could consider what we have lost or lost access to and see its importance to us. In modern times we consider *sadness* a "bad" emotion, and so we try to avoid it. In other words, we shrug off and ignore what may be important about it. We see *sadness as* "bothersome" or "annoying," but ontologically the claim is that those are not the reasons we experience it and those sensations are not random. *Sadness* comes to us to tell us something, and the question is whether we are wise enough to listen.

There seem to be two main reasons we try to avoid emotions. One is that some emotions are uncomfortable. *Sadness, anger, shame, embarrassment, despair,* and many others feel quite "bad" physically. Perhaps we have not understood the purpose of the discomfort. Our claim is that it is our body's way of alerting us to the emotion. If it did not feel "bad" (or in other cases "good"), we would not notice it or pay attention to it. It is a way of signaling us that an emotion is present. Another reason is the fear that we will "become stuck" in the emotion. In other words, that the emotion will morph into a mood and we will not be able to get out of it. With *sadness,* the fear is that we will drop into depression and not be able to escape. Perhaps this happens, but our experience is that attending to the emotions life is provoking in real time is an effective way of navigating them.

Trusting Emotions

Trust is the emotion that helps me assess risk. Given that emotions are not generally seen as reliable, I may want to ask if I am taking undue risk when I begin learning in this domain. At what level do you trust your emotions are giving you reliable information? Do you disregard them, trust them a little, or trust them 100 percent of the time? Our inclination in the past few centuries has been to place trust in reason, and because we've seen emotions as the opposite of reason, we have assumed they could not be relied upon. This is interesting, because many times we'll think or say, "I'm going to trust my gut on this one" or "I *knew* it was a mistake from the beginning." To a degree we all trust our emotions, but we implicitly know that there are aspects of emotions which we do not trust fully. We coordinate action with others, which shows we are in the emotion of *trust*. We marry based on our *love* or *passion*. Every choice we make has an emotional element to it. At the same time, we are often *skeptical* about *trusting* our emotions, and most of us feel we have been misled by them at times. The conclusion we draw from this is that there is a level at which our emotions are reliable guides in life, but that does not mean we should blindly believe everything they tell us. Doing so is in itself an emotion—*naiveté*.

If we look at the other domains that constitute us as humans, we might conclude we have a similar situation with them. Our reasoning cannot be said to be correct 100 percent of the time. If you place a pencil upright in a half glass of water, it will appear that the pencil is broken or exists in two pieces that are not aligned, but when you remove it, you will see it is whole. We often mix up things, confuse them, forget them, or just don't understand them fully. Perhaps if there is such a thing as pure reason, it is 100 percent reliable, but our reasoning clearly is not. The same is true of the feelings, impressions, and intuitions our bodies receive. When our foot falls asleep, it feels as if it is not there, but if we look, we will find it is.

The ontological perspective on this is that language, emotion, and body all contribute their part to our understanding of ourselves and the world around us. Each of the three is a gift if we choose to see it that way, and combining the input from the three will give us the most comprehensive understanding available.

Tools of Navigation

There are a number of tools, skills, or habits we can develop that allow us to be with our emotions and benefit from their wisdom.

- **Quiet time** in its many forms is one. Meditation, centering, or dedicated reflection allows us to quiet our thinking and notice our emotions, listen to them, and name them. Routines of many kinds—running, washing dishes by hand, sitting in a rocking chair on the porch—can quiet the mind and allow us to listen to our emotions, although the less active we are, the better.

- **Journaling**. If you journal as a way of speaking with yourself and listening, you will see patterns on reflection that cannot be seen when you are only thinking about your situation. Emotions will always be part of what we write, even if we need to look for them underneath the words.

- **Time**. We've spoken about the difference between *reacting* and *responding*. The primary thing that separates the two is time. When we "take a deep breath" or "count to ten" we are creating a break in time that allows us to move from *reacting* to *responding*. Sometimes we will need to count to ten more than once, but ultimately that space allows us to step back from reaction in order to consider our response. In this case, "sleeping on it" or "allowing time for the dust to settle" is a useful approach. The common factor in all of these is time.

■ **Conversation.** In social conversations, our aim is that the other person understands what we are experiencing in life. If I talk about my basement being flooded, I am trying to communicate the facts about the flooding and also to generate *empathy* in the other person. I'm hoping they "will feel what I feel." Or perhaps I'm aiming for *sympathy*, which means that at least they "understand how I feel." Two things can happen in these conversations. The first is that my friend, through trying to understand my experience, may ask questions or make comments that cause me to reflect on my emotions. The second is that hearing myself express my emotions may allow me to consider them differently than simply thinking about them. Other conversations may also help the navigation process. Counseling or therapeutic conversations, of course, are designed to do exactly this. Coaching is the authors' chosen medium, and in our experience, the most effective coaching conversations include an exploration of emotions at some level.

Listening to Our Emotions

Listening is a big part of understanding and navigating emotions. There are at least three distinct ways in which we can focus our listening distinct from hearing, which is the mechanical aspect. The first and most common is listening for *information*. This is discerning the "what" that is happening. Much of what we share with each other, much of what we teach, and the majority of news media focuses on this way of listening. The second level is to listen for *meaning*. In other words, we are focused on what the person intends for us to understand rather than on exactly what they are saying. This is what analysis of the news is all about. Listening for meaning is particularly important when we are in conversation with someone from a different cultural or work background. Meaning is at the root of why we try to communicate in the first place. The third way of listening is to listen to the *observer* that the other person is revealing. And in this we are listening for which emotions they are telling us they are in through the language they use.

For instance, if someone tells us they are angry with their boss, here is the way we would listen at each level:

- Information—We would focus on why our friend is angry. What did their boss do or not do? What about that "made" them angry?

- Meaning—We might inquire or listen for what it means to the person that their boss did or did not do something. If their boss skipped their performance review meeting, they might say it means their boss doesn't care about them, that with their boss they always come second or their boss is scared to share his or her assessments with them.

- Observer—Listening to the observer that the person is, we would discern from the story that they believe they are not important to their boss and that their evidence is the lack of their boss's attention. This might mean that they do not have a strong relationship with *dignity*, which is the story that "I am enough." We know that because a person in the emotion of *dignity* does not need the acknowledgment of others, even if they would like to have it. At this level of listening we cannot be absolutely sure of what we see, but we can verify it with the speaker.

The ability to navigate the emotions that arise in daily life requires that we understand the basic concept of emotions as predispositions to action and that we build an understanding of the stories connected with specific questions. Some of this is simply memorization, just as we learned the multiplication table. Beyond that, it is a matter of listening deeply and reflecting on the experience of our own emotions. The following are a few examples of situations of emotional navigation:

Examples

Story #1. Anger: One day recently I was walking through the city where I live. I wasn't aware of what I was thinking, but after a bit I realized that I felt *angry*. I could feel my energy rising, heat in my face, my breathing got shallow, and I felt like lashing out. When I noticed these sensations and realized they were signaling *anger*, I got *curious*. Nothing had happened on my walk that would have provoked *anger*. As I reflected I realized that my thoughts—more like daydreams, actually—had been about a situation where I thought that someone who owed me money for my work was probably not going to pay me as promised. This was fascinating. Nothing, so far, had happened except my thoughts about the possibility that I wouldn't be paid as promised. So up to the moment nothing unjust had been done, but I was anticipating there might be. That thought about "potential future injustice" triggered my emotion of *anger*. And in the emotion of *anger* I was imagining how I might punish the transgressor.

As I reflected, consciously now, about what the *anger* was trying to tell me, it occurred to me that it could be alerting me to the possibility that the thing might occur and that I would consider it unjust. As a precaution, I could take steps to be sure that the other person's commitment was firm and would be fulfilled. I also realized that the other person probably had no idea about my concern, and to approach them in *anger* would not be productive. I decided the best solution was simply to email to double-check on our agreement and terms. My reason for writing was that I was doing some planning and needed to be sure, as part of my plan depended on this payment, which was true.

For me, this is an example of navigation. I could have gotten caught up in the *anger* and reacted, which would not have been productive. I could have moved to other emotions, such as *resentment* ("I shouldn't <u>have</u> to check") or *resignation* ("There is nothing I can do about it") or even *naïveté* ("I'm sure it will all work out"), but I don't think any of them would have been as effective. Navigation then is (1) becoming aware of your emotion, (2) listening to and understanding your emotion, (3) questioning the source of your emotion, (4) choosing another emotion that can help you "avoid the rocks" and move forward effectively.

Story #2. Forgiveness: Some years ago I was asked by a woman to coach her on something she had struggled with for many years. She told me that she had been unable to *forgive* herself for something that had happened a decade before. The story she shared was that she and her partner had a son together and that he had health challenges through childhood. When he was five years old, he became ill with a fever while she was traveling for work. Based on her partner's descriptions, she dismissed her son's illness as routine and continued her travels. When she arrived home, she discovered her son's fever was worse than she understood and took him to urgent care. It was only after his recovery that it was discovered that the high fever had damaged his hearing.

She blamed herself for not investigating more deeply and blamed her partner for what she saw as his casual approach to their son's health. Her statement to me was that no matter what she did since that time, she "felt guilt toward her son and could not forgive herself or her partner."

Chapter 6: Navigating Emotions

This is an experience none of us would wish on another, but it is something that does happen in life, and unless we are willing to remain in a state of suffering, we need to find a way to navigate it. Clearly the woman was "stuck." *Blame, regret, shame, guilt,* and *anger* are all emotions that were likely part of her being stuck, but the emotion that she was unable to generate was *forgiveness.* And that is the emotion she identified both in regard to herself and her former partner.

If we take a look at *forgiveness* from the ontological point of view, we can deconstruct:

- The story: "I believe something you have done has injured me, but I promise I will not use it against you in future interactions."
- The predisposition: To accept that something did occur, but not to forget it or its impact and not use it against the other.
- The purpose: *Forgiveness* allows us to live with the reality of our experience without the need to punish.

In this case, the story was that both she and her partner had done something to hurt their child, and furthermore that she had ignored characteristics of her own and of her partner that were the cause. What she had been searching for in vain was *self-forgiveness.* Her interpretation was that *forgiveness* included "forgetting," and she even said at one point that she "couldn't forget" what they had done. Considering the possibility that she did not need to forget what happened to their son in order to *forgive* herself or her former partner was a new interpretation for her. We can well imagine the trap that her belief created for her.

The woman's reported outcome was a shift in her understanding of forgiveness and an ability to embrace and practice it in order to allow her to move ahead in life. This is the possibility of developing a new inter-pretation of emotions. The *blame, regret, shame, guilt,* and *anger* were also all trying to deliver messages, but in the confusion of those there was no path to *forgiveness* for her or her former partner. *Forgiveness* in this interpretation must include remembering and is simply a commitment to stop punishing yourself for past behavior.

Story #3. Shame: I worked with a man who was director of business development in a company of about 200 people. He was extremely well liked and respected by almost everyone and he was successful in his role. He was happily married and had a son of eight he was obviously proud of. In our conversation he shared with me privately that even though he could recognize that others liked him and trusted him, that his family loved him, and that he was successful in most things he did, he couldn't shake the feeling that there was something "wrong" with him. He felt that all of that outward success contrasted with an inward feeling of inadequacy.

As we explored his life and self-doubt, he began to connect it to his feeling that he often felt like hiding. Listening to the observer he was, it occurred to me that the predisposition to hide is often connected with the emotion of *shame*. Ontologically the story of *shame* is that "I have broken the rules or standards of the community." When asked if he might be feeling *shame,* he couldn't imagine anything he had done that might be a source. When we explored his first awareness of this, he realized that even before he had the desire to hide himself, he had a desire to hide his father. It turned out his father was Asian, and among his friends this was unique. The man I was working with did not have physical features that would suggest he was Asian American, and he said he could remember not wanting his friends to know that his father was Asian, because it was different from their fathers and he was afraid of being rejected. What we arrived at was that he felt *shame* about his father not because of anything his father had done but because of who his father was. In that moment he reported feeling *shame* for wanting to hide his father when he was a child. In essence he felt *shame* about his previous *shame*. The resolution was quite simple, which was for him to talk with his father about his experiences growing up as a child and that it was not in any way connected with his love.

For me this example is very powerful, because sometimes we feel an emotion like *shame* not because of what we have done but because of our story of who we are. Another important aspect is that we often feel emotions about our emotions, and this can complicate listening to their meaning. If it is a case of feeling *shame* about feeling *anger,* it is likely that we will live in the *shame* without ever discovering or exploring the meaning of the *anger*. We develop the emotions we need to take care of ourselves when we are young. As in this case, sometimes those emotions do not serve who we have become as adults. Discovering this and making conscious choices about which emotions will best support us allows us to move through life with more ease.

Story #4. Impatience: How do we know what emotion we are experiencing when two feel similar? For instance, *sadness* and *despair*. Or *anxiety* and *doubt*. Ontologically it can be determined by the story or what we are thinking at the time of the emotion.

A woman I worked with who was in her late thirties kept telling me how *impatient* she was and how she wished she could change that aspect of her character because she didn't like it. When I asked her what she was feeling when she was "impatient," she said she had a great desire to get out and do things, take on big tasks, go on adventures, and do challenging things. When I asked her what she was thinking in those moments, she said that she thought the world was a big and fascinating place and she wanted to experience all she could of it. To me that did not sound like *impatience*, which is the story that "things should be moving faster" or "I'm wasting my time doing this." When I asked how she knew the emotion she was experiencing was *impatience*, she said that is what her parents called it. The situation turned out to be that she was the oldest of five children, gifted with tremendous energy, and was always asking to go do things with the family. Her parents' response was to tell her to "quit being so impatient." When talking about what other emotion she might be experiencing if it wasn't *impatience*, she named both *enthusiasm* and *exuberance*. As it turned out, these matched her energy and thoughts much more closely than *impatience* and allowed her to shift her assessment of herself from something she had held as a negative to something she felt positive about. There are other emotions she could have named, such as *elation, ebullience,* or *adventurousness,* and each has its own distinct story. Possibly she was experiencing a combination of these, and the point is not to identify one as the "correct" emotion but to see the field on which she is playing out her life.

This misnaming of emotions is quite common. We confuse *shame* and *guilt,* lack a distinction between *service* and *sacrifice,* and cannot distinguish among *fear, anxiety,* and *doubt.* When we cannot distinguish what emotion is present, we cannot understand what it is trying to communicate to us or choose an effective path to navigate it. We are handicapped by our ignorance.

Story #5. Trust: By default, most of us learned that to trust or not trust was somehow a judgment of character. It was connected with whether we thought the other person was a good or bad person. In that sense it can be seen as a moral issue. This, of course, makes it nearly impossible to talk about, because it would be heard as accusing the other person of being of bad character. Trust has also not been seen as something we can learn and change. There are two stories about my family that can illustrate this. When my son was about twelve years old, he would beg me to allow him to drive the car. Perhaps it was only in the driveway, but he deeply wanted to begin driving. I declined his request because I did not trust him as a driver. If we take the ontological interpretation of *trust,* it makes sense. Trust is the emotion that "allows us to interact with others" and it is an assessment constituted of sincerity, competence, and reliability. My determination was that he was completely sincere that he wouldn't crash the car, but that he had never demonstrated his competence, nor did he have a history of reliability in driving. So I decided not to "coordinate action" with him. In no way did I think of him as a bad character; I absolutely loved him and wanted to support his learning. However, based on the emotion of *trust,* which in this case was low, I could not allow it. Later, after he took his training with me and with a professional, I assessed he had the sincerity and competence to drive, and from then on I *trusted* him at least with the basics. As his history of reliability extended, my *trust* grew, and I had fewer and fewer reservations. This is an example of how trust evolves over time if we continue to check our assessments.

By contrast, when my stepfather was about eighty years old, after sixty years of accident-free driving, he began to scrape his van against the garage door frame. Other small accidents and near misses occurred, and one day, using the *trust* model, it became clear to the family that even though he was absolutely sincere about driving safely, there was mounting evidence (history of reliability) that his competence had diminished. The result was that we asked him to surrender his keys and to become a passenger rather than a driver. The transition was very difficult for him, but in the end he agreed.

This is an example again of checking our assessments to see what has changed so that we can be prudent in extending *trust*. In this case, our choice again had nothing to do with the quality of his character or morality, but only that it was deemed imprudent to allow him to continue driving.

Emotional learning shifts relationships

I was having a breakdown and struggling a great deal in my relationship with one of my relatives. I had a story about this person that "blinded" me to the anger and unfairness I was really feeling. Because I loved and admired him, I believed I couldn't also be angry or disappointed with him. My coach helped me understand the difference between admiration (having a desire to be like they are) and worship (putting them on a higher plane). I realized that I could choose to reframe the way I saw him and that would allow me to have a more honest and satisfying relationship. The basis of the choice needed to be the emotion in which I held him. The net result was an emotional shift within myself which allowed me to request conversations that respected both of us, giving me the ability to live in integrity with greater ease and grace.

—H.A.

Chapter 7

EMOTIONS IN DAILY LIFE

Noticing Emotions

The next time you are standing in line waiting for service, notice what is happening to you emotionally. What sensations or feelings are you experiencing? What stories are they connected to? If you notice that the other lines are moving more quickly than yours, what emotion and story are provoked? You might feel *regret* if you are thinking you should have chosen another line. If you are thinking the situation is unfair, you are experiencing *resentment,* and if you believe it is unjust, you are *angry*. Or you could simply *accept* that the lines are moving as they are, that you will get served in good time, and that there was no way to guess which line would be faster. The point is that you are always experiencing an emotion—"in an emotion," as we sometimes say—and that emotion is connected with your thoughts or stories. It doesn't matter if you are expressing any of these emotions by changing lines, asking the clerk to hurry up, or drumming your fingers; you are still experiencing the emotions themselves.

Once you begin to notice that "you are never not in an emotion," they will take on a different dimension in your life. Suddenly they become core

167

to every thought or action. We could truthfully say that no human action happens without emotions. A physical comparison could be if you were to notice the existence and presence of water. It comes out of the tap, falls out of the sky, and we use it to wash, to cook, to clean, to slake our thirst, and water our plants. It is in the air as humidity and makes up a majority of our bodies. And yet we often overlook its importance, its absolute necessity for supporting human life. As with water, we cannot appreciate the value of emotions or treat them with respect until we see their prevalence and our dependence on them.

How and where emotions show up in life varies widely. In different stages of life, we have different relationships with emotions and with particular emotions, but they are a nondiscretionary aspect of being human.

Learning Emotions

If we believe that the emotional domain is not fixed, it is logical to think that we are born with the potential to understand emotions, but there is learning to be done. Just as babies are born with a certain amount of physical or cognitive ability, so it is with emotions, and day by day we add to all three sets of abilities. How we grow in the three areas is substantially different. We learn intellectually through insight. That is to say that cognitive learning happens when we see something that fits into our current understanding of how the world works and it "makes sense" to us. It can also happen when something does not fit, and we revise our understanding to include it. This happens when we learn that storks do not actually deliver babies and that Christmas presents are not left by Santa Claus. The cognitive dissonance of information that does not fit our understanding produces the emotion of *confusion,* which challenges us to find a new way of understanding.

Physically or somatically, we learn by repetition. This explains why even very skilled athletes continue to practice the fundamentals of their sport. It is not just that they don't want to "forget" how to move, but they want to continue to refine their somatic learning. It is why we must practice piano in order to improve (learn) and why understanding music cognitively is not sufficient to make us pianists. It may not be that "practice makes perfect," but it can be said that "practice produces learning."

Emotionally we learn through immersion, and this is key to understanding how we develop in the emotional domain. In this context, "immersion" means that we are "plunged into" or "dipped into" emotions. This can happen by living in a certain emotional context. If we grow up in a home we perceive to be dangerous for us in some way, we will learn *fear*. In a different home we might learn *service* or *ambition*, depending on the emotional context. The part of the brain responsible for emotions, the limbic system, learns through this immersion. Being immersed in this context also means "allowing ourselves to experience our emotions." An analogy might be that when we are out riding our bicycle, we are getting exercise, but we are also improving our ability to ride. Without the riding, we cannot deepen our embodied knowing. Without experiencing our emotions, we cannot deepen our understanding of them.

Conscious learning happens in three steps:

These apply well to the choice to learn in the emotional domain. First, you can become aware of many distinctions about emotions by reading this book and other sources. Second, you will need to choose if emotions are something you commit to studying and learning. Third, you will need to develop practices.

Laughter and Crying

Our bodies are the container for our emotions. We experience our emotions through the feelings or sensations our bodies offer and through our thoughts/stories which occur in the brain, also part of the body. Just as our brains have a capacity to think, our bodies have a capacity to experience emotions. Learning algebra (or statistics or chemistry) required your brain to expand its capacity. Learning in the emotional domain had a similar effect. This growth or expansion occurs when we practice. We practice thinking in new ways to expand our cognitive capacity, and we practice emoting in new ways to expand our emotional capacity. When we do not have the capacity to understand something intellectually, it often produces mental confusion. When we do not have the capacity for a strong or sudden emotion, our body reacts either by laughing or crying. Ontologically that is the meaning of the two. Either the emotion was generated so suddenly that we did not have time to experience it or we did not have the capacity to "hold" the emotion. If you notice, children have what we could think of as a "small emotional container," and even small events will provoke tears (or laughter). As we grow, our capacity expands, often without direct effort, and crying or laughing is only provoked by larger events.

This distinction is a valuable alternative to the story that "crying demonstrates weakness." That, like our traditional interpretation of *trust*, has a moral basis rather than a practical one. Crying and laughter are releases, but they also tell us something important about our emotional capacity. As with other aspects of emotions and moods we can, over time, build or learn to have more capacity in this domain.

Emotions and Action

The understanding of emotions as "E-Motions" or "that which puts us in motion" is fundamental. In this context "motion" and "action" should not be confused. In an emotion such as *contentment* or *acceptance* or even in suppressed *anger*, we may not demonstrate any action, or very little. *Action* means "performing" or "doing." To move means to "guide or direct." We can be moved without taking action. Every emotion has a particular "pre" disposition, meaning it is "guiding" or "directing" us toward a specific action that we may or may not take. "Being with" a particular emotion therefore does not necessarily mean to act it out. In this awareness lies the foundation of responding vs. reacting to an emotion.

Emotions and Planning

At first it may seem as if there is not a strong relationship between emotions and planning, as we usually think of planning as a rational activity. Planning means choosing our priorities, putting them in order, and assigning times when we will do them. That is true, but ignores the essence of what is needed for us to "prioritize." If "to prioritize" means "to put in order of importance," the question is how we know or determine what is most important. That determination is a function of emotions. *Urgency* will result in one list and order, while *service* will result in another, and *prudence* yet another. In a sense, you could say that we "see" the list through the filter of the emotion or mood we are in. So the complete activity of planning is a joint effort of reason and emotions. We collect data and information using reason and filter it through emotions in order to develop a plan.

There is also a nuance between emotions and moods as the filter of our choices. Remember that one key distinction between the two is that moods precede our understanding and actions and emotions are reactions or responses to events. So someone living in the mood of *ambition* will see the world as full of possibilities and will plan accordingly. Someone living in the mood of *resignation* will see no possibilities and will plan from there. Planning from *resentment* will include a way to "get even" for something we believe was unfair, while planning from *service* will include doing helpful things for other people. When you begin to prepare a plan, whether it is for vacation, starting a business, or making a movie, it is worthwhile to consider the mood in which you are making that plan, as it will have a strong impact on the outcome.

Speaking and Emotion

Since language is ultimately a function of the body, and emotions are what put the body in action, it follows that we cannot think or speak without emotions playing their parts. So the very act of speaking is fueled by emotion. Asking a question is fueled by *curiosity*; arguing against a planned action could come from *care, fear, prudence,* or any number of other emotions. Furthermore, specific statements in language point directly to specific emotions. Telling your child to be careful is fueled by *love,* and declaring you will travel around the world by *adventurousness, ambition,* or *pride.*

Why bother?

If we want to build expertise in the domain of emotions, we need to understand the distinctions we have already covered, but to connect those distinctions with our personal lives we need to be able to identify our own emotions. Most of us were never taught how to do this, and so we might not be very good at it. When I was a boy I can remember wanting to learn to identify all the different brands and models of automobiles. My brothers and I would take turns calling out the name, model, and year of the cars we saw on the road, and we would either agree on or argue about what we thought the other person had wrong. As silly a game as it was, it helped us to learn distinctions, even small ones, between similar cars to the point that knowing what we were seeing was automatic. This method also turns out to be useful for learning to distinguish emotions and build a vocabulary. Since shouting out emotions to people around you might be seen as a bit strange, a better method is to write down your emotion several times each day and reflect on how you identified that was the emotion you were feeling. If you cannot name one emotion exactly, you can put several or write the one you believe is closest. If you continue this exercise on a regular basis for several weeks, you will notice that you recognize and use a growing list. Listening to other people and being curious what emotion they are speaking from also helps. In the end, the number of distinctions you have about emotions determines your knowledge or expertise, as in any other field.

Observing my emotions

I am a coach and have found that in coaching conversations, there is sometimes initial reluctance to acknowledge the significance of emotion, if not the very existence of emotion as an element of life. Helping coachees recognize the existence of emotions and then focusing on the events that evoke those emotions has been a powerful tool. The most impactful aspect of the emotions workshop for me was being invited to take the time to sit in the emotion, whether on a bench in the forest or in a yurt in the presence of others in order to more deeply understand the emotion and its impact.

This allowed me to understand the deeper aspects of a particular emotion—joy, fear, or anxiety, for example—and through increased awareness choose which were beneficial or not to me. I now practice mindful contemplation to embrace the lessons my emotions can teach me, and I am able to help others approach life's challenges from an emotionally aware mindset. Feeling change through emotional awareness adds invaluable depth to a conversation about change. This is a methodology I now use with my coachees. I've realized that many times I do not need to "teach" emotions directly in order for my coachees to learn, but simply help them recognize and listen to their emotions for a change to happen.

—K.M.

When expectations meet reality

As my daughter entered her adolescent years, she suddenly became belligerent, unreasonable, and accusatory. I had no idea how to handle this change in her, and it produced feelings of incompetence in me as a parent as well as sadness over the loss of my "angel of a daughter." One day I was feeling particularly overwrought about the dynamic that was developing between my daughter and me. That day on a group coaching call I "raised my hand" to be coached by Dan. As I began to articulate my frustration that "it shouldn't be happening like this," Dan asked me questions that challenged my assumptions: "When you say it 'shouldn't be happening this way,' what is the standard you have for that? What's the story about why it shouldn't be this way? What is creating your expectations?"

The story that emerged was that I believed if I was a good mother, my daughter and I would get through the teenage years without such turbulence. I had struggled tremendously as a teenager and believed that it was due in large part to my parents not being present, either physically or emotionally. Therefore, if I was present for my daughter in ways that my parents weren't present for me, she wouldn't have to struggle. And because she was struggling, I was obviously failing as a parent. It felt ludicrous to put this into words. But there it was.

Dan explained about expectations and disappointment. How we are always making up a story about how the future "should" be, and if reality doesn't match our expectations, we experience the emotion of disappointment. I was disappointed because the story I'd made up about how it was going to be during my daughter's teen years wasn't what was happening. I learned that when expectations meet reality, reality wins. In reality, teenagers often struggle, no matter what type of parenting they get. My story was generating the powerful emotions I was experiencing. If I could change the story, the emotions could change too. Instead of my story being "I'm disappointed because this isn't how it was supposed to be during her teen years," I shifted to "I am in fact a good mother, and her struggle is part of what teenagers experience as they grow up. It's normal." My daughter continued to be as hormone-ridden an adolescent as you can imagine, but my story changed, and along with it my emotions about my parenting and myself.

—B.K.

Chapter 8

EMOTIONS IN THE WIDE WORLD

U p until now you may have found the ideas and distinctions we've presented interesting. We, the authors, find that in coaching and teaching
emotions, the most challenging step for most people is seeing emotions in
all they do and connecting their learning with their daily experiences. In this
section we link emotions and moods to some key parts of life. When we can
see how moods and emotions fuel these areas or give them direction, we can
begin to see the enormous power of the emotional domain in all we do as
human beings.

Organizations

We can think of an organization as "a group of two or more people who
join together to do something they could not do individually." So what is it
that "joins them together"? Within organizations we talk in terms of vision
or purpose or enlightened self-interest to explain this bond, but a powerful
way of understanding this dynamic is through the energy of emotions. The
most critical emotion in any organization is *trust*. *Trust*, as we've seen, is the

emotion that allows us to coordinate action with others. It is inconceivable for an organization to exist without it, which tells us that whenever we find an organization, there is some level of *trust*, no matter how weak it may be. A weak organization still relies on *trust*, but that *trust* is at a low level.

Trust, of course, is necessary among co-workers, but is also highly relevant to the concept of organizations in other ways. When there is a serious challenge to the *trust* customers have in an organization or its products, it needs to be treated as the highest of priorities. In 1982 when several people in Chicago died from Tylenol capsules that had been tampered with, Johnson & Johnson immediately recalled 31 million bottles with a retail value of $100 million at their own expense. They advertised for consumers to avoid their own products, which the day before they had been promoting. They quickly established that the tampering had happened within stores and not on their production lines. They offered customers replacement Tylenol in solid form as a substitute for the capsules, and with tamper-proof packaging. Johnson & Johnson was acknowledged by many to have done the "right" thing, and most of us would not argue with that assessment, but if you look beyond their commercial interests or ethical commitments to the reason their actions were so important, you will find the emotion of *trust*. Their main concern was that customers would continue or return to "coordinating action" with them. Within a year of the incidents, Tylenol was once again the largest seller in its category. That is the value of *trust*.[2]

The history of the growth and changes in the auto industry is another area that is intimately connected with *trust*. When Japanese cars were entering the American market in the 1960s, the manufacturers needed to establish that their cars were reliable. Over the decades that is what they focused

---

2 "Chicago Tylenol Murders," *Wikipedia*, https://en.wikipedia.org/wiki/Chicago_Tylenol_murders.

on, to the point that Toyota and Honda became the most reliable vehicles in the world. They needed to convince customers that a 4-cylinder engine was as durable and reliable as a 6- or 8-cylinder engine, which was the norm at the time. The success of Toyota in the U.S. market is spoken about in many ways, but fundamentally it is based on a growing assessment of *trust* among consumers. Without a sufficient level of *trust,* people would not have "coordinated action," which in this case was demonstrated by buying cars. In contrast, the current situation VW finds itself in is also a matter of trust. It turns out that VW did not build the diesel engine they claimed, and they hid the fact. Since *trust* is built on sincerity, competence, and reliability, they managed to diminish all three and have seen consumers' willingness to interact with them decrease and suspicion increase.

Another emotion that is a regular feature of organizations is *loyalty*. Loyalty is the emotion that predisposes us to take care of the boundaries of the group. In organizations there can be *loyalty* to the vision, structure, leader, or products. The particular "group" an employee sees himself or herself a part of will determine what flavor of *loyalty* they have and who or what they will defend. *Loyalty*, while a necessary emotion in organizations, isn't necessarily beneficial in every case. An employee who is blindly *loyal* to a corrupt leader will support the leader, but to the detriment of the organization, team, or public. An employee who is *loyal* to the organization may fight against or resist their boss, which could have negative consequences for their career.

Other emotions that are often found creating or sustaining organizations include *fear* (that the organization might fail and that we employees might lose our livelihoods), *pride* (the belief that we have done something good and want to tell others about it), *satisfaction* (the sense that we have enough—success, for instance—and are thus content), or *passion* (we are deeply immersed in what we are doing and love it for the sake of doing it). Of course, it is possible for any of the several hundred emotions to show up in an organization, and at times they will, but understanding the most common ones can help us know what might be missing and help us focus on generating the emotions that move the organization in the desired direction.

Moods, being the underlying energy, have a different role in organizations. Moods inform our interpretation of experiences, so an organization living in the mood of *ambition* would see a world full of possibilities and want to take advantage of them. The mood of *gravitas* or *gravity* will result in you taking yourselves and your mission seriously, while *service* will have the mission to take care of others' well-being. If it's the mood, it means it is present in all the conversations and activities of the organization, often unconsciously. A misalignment between the mood and organizational activities will prevent success. It is difficult to imagine a company in the mood of *shame* being able to promote its services and products effectively.

Leadership

If you consider the role of any leader, it is to move his or her organization from the present into the future. Generally, we think of good leaders as those who can do this by generating a vision of the future that others get *enthusiastic* about and want to help create. Unless the leader's role is tasked with closing an organization, we tend to associate leadership with growth and sustainability. Underneath each of these ideas we could identify specific behaviors—clear communication, a coherent vision, active engagement—and each of those behaviors rests on a foundation of particular emotions. *Respect, enthusiasm, care,* or *inspiration* are all good candidates.

When facing a particular challenge, it can be said that fundamentally the leader's job is "to generate the mood or emotion within the organization that will take care of the task at hand." *Fear, urgency,* or *competition,* as well as *loyalty, pride, or enthusiasm* can all be of value when they generate the actions needed in that moment. The adept leader, whether intuitively or deliberately, depends on emotions to move himself or herself as well as his team. We often think about strong leaders as movers and shakers or as charismatic, but do not often take the next step to examine the source of these attributes.

Politics

We generally think of politics as being driven by beliefs—liberal, conservative, socialist, democratic, Marxist, libertarian—and almost exclusively focus our attention there when considering candidates. Beliefs, however, are simply stories that co-create certain emotions. For instance, if we live the mood of *prudence*, particularly in terms of our financial resources, we might lean toward the conservative viewpoint of maintaining a small government that is fiscally responsible. If we live strongly in the mood of *compassion,* we might moderate that position and consider a larger government that could provide more social services to people with a demonstrated need. In this example, what underpins our political beliefs are the emotions of *prudence* and *compassion.* If we *fear* for personal safety, we might find comfort with the idea of a larger police force, fire department, or military. However, if our *fear* is of government interference in our lives or intimidation, our beliefs might lean toward libertarianism. In short, it is the moods and emotions predominant in our lives that have us taking the view we do politically.

As a political leader it is no different, and the fact that we have chosen politics as our vocation will be closely linked with our personal emotions. Otto Von Bismarck is quoted as saying that "Politics is the art of the possible." If we start from his definition, the obvious question is "Which emotions open possibilities?" If *service* is my mood in life, I will be a servant leader. If *greed* is dominant, I will look for the financial advantages I might gain from a political position. Being a political leader could be linked to a strong personal mood of *ambition* to be the best nation/state/city we can, *enthusiasm* for the possibilities we can generate, *hope* for our future, *arrogance* that I will lead better than anyone else might, or *dignity* for each of us as legitimate citizens.

Also, given the complexity of the political environment due to constant change, *trust* stands as the emotion that connects one with the purpose and the impact that our actions as politicians have on others. If *love* is the ability to hold the other as legitimate, it has a central place in politics that claim to be "of the people and for the people." True conversations begin with the *acceptance* of the other's legitimacy. It is enlightening to consider even politics and political philosophies through the lens of emotions as a means of deeper understanding.

Science

When the scientific method was a school topic, it was based on the proposition that science was "value-free and impartial." We learned that to be those things a scientist needed to be "objective" in his or her thinking and experiments. These ideas or standards were attempts to make science less prone to people's preexisting beliefs and open to consider whatever evidence could be unearthed through study. The idea of being *objective* (judgment based on observable phenomena and uninfluenced by emotions or personal prejudices) was based on the idea that one could be the observer of something without also influencing it or becoming a part of it.[3] On the scale and with the tools available when the scientific method was proposed, it seemed that *objectivity* was possible and all we needed to do was to be rigorous about maintaining it. Perhaps the distinction missing was that a *process* might be objective but that the *person* creating and experimenting could not be. The emergence of quantum theory has demonstrated that objectivity as we previously understood it is not possible. The observer of the experiment will always influence the experiment because he or she is a particular observer. That shift also implies that those people practicing science do not do so from an emotionless state.

Clearly no science would happen without the emotion of *curiosity*. Sometimes, as in the case of a public health crisis, *urgency* may be driving the study. *Care* or *service* is often part of the mix, but fundamental to all science is the emotion of *skepticism*. Since *skepticism* is the emotion that allows us to distinguish what we will believe (in that it fits with our understanding of the world) and what we will not believe, it is essential to scientific inquiry. It is the emotion that has us asking if we are sure that "x causes y" and if there is a way to be more certain. It is also the emotion that compels us to seek evidence that is logically irrefutable. No sphere of human activity is outside of emotions, because humans are emotional beings. We could say that emotions are a part, an element, of all human activities because they are a part of every human. The question again is not whether they are "good or bad" emotions but rather what they allow us to do and what they do not allow. In the case of science, *skepticism* is a central emotion that made it possible

3 "Objectivity," *The Free Dictionary*, http://www.thefreedictionary.com/objectivity.

and has made it so successful. In that sense and in that context, it has been a gift, but we should be careful not to assume it is in any way superior to any other emotion.

Psychology

Partly as an outgrowth of the trust we put into thinking in a scientific manner, we found an increasing number of ways to apply it to more and more areas of human experience. One of these was medicine, or "the science and art of diagnosing and treating disease or injury and maintaining health."[4] Within medicine we focused attention on "the science that deals with mental processes and behavior" and employed it to try to understand "the emotional and behavioral characteristics of an individual, group, or activity," which we called psychology.[5] By this path, emotions ended up within the domain of psychology. In the West in particular we are quite attached, at least by habit, to having them there. Whenever we begin to look at emotions as an area of study we generally default to psychology and its extended studies in counseling and psychotherapy because this has been our traditional understanding.

The claim the authors make is that while this has been and is useful in building, understanding, and learning about the emotional field, it is also restrictive. Emotions and moods exist outside of psychology, and because psychology is based on a way of observing that is based in science, it can only see emotions from one perspective. That makes it blind to other

---

4 "Medicine," *American Heritage Dictionary*, 5th ed., http://www.thefreedictionary.com/medicine.
5 "Psychology," *American Heritage Dictionary*, 5th ed., http://www.thefreedictionary.com/psychology.

interpretations that may be useful for us to consider. The ontological interpretation that has been presented is one such way. The core distinction between viewing emotions from a traditional psychological perspective and an ontological one is that the psychological view was based on the medical model, which includes an ill patient and a doctor who is trying to cure that illness, while the ontological model is simply based in learning. It is an epistemological model and is not designed to address illness but only to explore our knowledge and understanding of emotions. It is also aimed at practicality, meaning that people educated in this interpretation of emotions will better understand themselves and thus be more capable of navigating life independently.

The authors want to be absolutely clear that in our view this in no way diminishes the value of psychology or its commitment to understand and work with emotions. Both authors have been the beneficiaries of psychological intervention, so experientially can confirm its value. At the same time, we can confirm the value of the ontological approach. We understand that the idea of studying and understanding emotions outside of psychology may trigger certain emotions. *Incredulity, skepticism,* and *doubt* come to mind as possibilities. We would also offer *hope, enthusiasm,* and *curiosity.* We do not believe it is an "either/or" situation, and this book is an invitation to build our collective understanding of emotions in a way that makes them practical tools in daily life for all of us.

Money

We tend to think that the phenomenon of money is largely mathematical, probably because we express it numerically. However, many financial planners teach that people's relationship with money is mostly emotional. We each have a story about money. If that story is that "the love of money is the root of all evil" (as proposed in the Bible, 1 Timothy 6:10), we may experience the emotions of *disgust, distaste,* or *disapproval* when we deal with money, and this will predispose us to avoid interacting with it. We might have the story that "money makes the world go round," in which case the emotions of *delight, ambition,* or *excitement* will predispose us to approach money in a different way. What we can derive from this is that understanding money has mostly to do with the relationship we have with it based on our stories and emotions.

Organized Religion

Religion means to recognize and be committed to living in a manner consistent with the desire of a higher power or powers. There are two foundational moods for religion: *faith* and *reverence. Faith* means we *trust* in something even when we do not have any evidence it is true. We can have *faith* in a god, the universe, life, other people, ourselves, science, nature. In other words, *faith* is not limited to either the material or immaterial. The predisposition of *faith* is to believe regardless of evidence. It allows humans to operate in a larger space than that defined by material evidence. Having *faith* in something does not mean it is either true or The Truth, but only that we believe we can rely on it supporting us and do not need proof to support our belief. *Reverence* means that we are in *awe* of the thing we revere. These two moods and the particular higher power we believe in shape our religious practices.

Advertising and Marketing

Looking at marketing and advertising through the lens of emotions reveals that emotions are the primary tool used to drive consumer actions. Sometimes the emotions are expressed directly:

- "I'm *lovin'* it" (McDonald's)
- "Open *Happiness*" (Coke)
- "*Happiness* is not around the corner; *happiness* is the corner" (BMW)
- "Passion Wins" (BMW)
- "*Loyalty* Programs Should Be *Loyal*" (Delta)
- "*Jooooy*" (Audi)
- "*Awe. Inspiring.*" (Mercedes-Benz)

Other times they are insinuated or suggested:

- "Impossible Is Nothing" (Adidas)—*Inspiration*
- "Where Do You Want To Go Today?" (Microsoft)—*Adventure*
- "Helps Your Work, Rest and Play" (Mars)—*Service*
- "Just Do It" (Nike)—*Ambition*
- "Diamonds Are a Girl's Best Friend" (Cartier)—*Loyalty*
- "We Try Harder" (Avis)—*Persistence*

Slogans suggesting that your product has the most features or is the most stylish or that our health care will help you avoid pain are all based on the essential driver of emotions. Different categories have their preferred and most useful emotions. *Fear* and *disgust* are often employed in ads to change self-destructive behavior like smoking cigarettes or illicit drugs like meth, *enjoyment* for personal goods, and *passion* for goods we want others to admire us for. The value of understanding emotions specifically is that we can decode the message of the marketing in the moment and understand how it is influencing us. If so, we can reground ourselves in our own beliefs and emotions to make our choices from center. If we get pulled into *urgent* action by a notice that tells us there are "only three seats remaining" or "30 other people reserved at this hotel in the past 24 hours," we may not be making the best choice for ourselves. We commonly call this "thinking for ourselves," but it is more in the vein of "emoting for ourselves." Teaching this to our children is doubly important, as they do not have the same powers of rational and emotional discrimination we do as adults to choose what to believe.

Consumerism

Around 1965 the word consumerism came to mean "encouraging consumption as an economic policy."[6] Since then it has been common to refer to ourselves as consumers and for shopping to be a common form of entertainment. How is that related to emotions? One way is that buying and having material things is driven by emotions. We feel that we can better weather the vagaries of life if we have food in the freezer or shoes in the closet, so we feel *safer*. Shopping is often an antidote for *boredom* and is promoted through the encouragement of *dissatisfaction* or *excitement,* and is sometimes even linked to being a *loyal* citizen. Since *boredom* is the emotion that tells

6 "Consumerism," *Online Etymology Dictionary,* http://www.etymonline.com/index. php?term=consumerism.

us "there is nothing here of value to me," we are inclined to buy something new, which is what makes us consumers.

Culture

The authors believe that culture can be understood as "a specific way a group understands and meets life's challenges." Whether we live in a family group, business, neighborhood, state, nation, or religious community, the kinds of interactions that are expected or acceptable, our rhythm of meals, and our relationship with the material and spiritual worlds are defined by culture. So a culture is defined by the spoken and unspoken rules of any group, and these rules emerge from similarity of worldviews.

The primary emotion associated with culture is *loyalty*. This is the emotion that signifies that I see myself as part of a group and will, if necessary, defend the boundaries of the group. Other emotions that play a part in culture include *trust* and *ease*. Just as there are emotions that generate culture, there are emotions that maintain culture. Chief among these is *shame*. The story of *shame* is that "I am aware that I have broken the rules of the community." If I am not aware or don't acknowledge that I have crossed any cultural boundaries, I will not feel *shame*. The rules I have broken may or may not be explicit and they may be spoken or unspoken. The intense discomfort of *shame* keeps us following the rules of the group we belong to, whether it is ethnic, national, organizational, or spiritual.

When we examine culture's relationship to moods and emotions, we're often looking not at moods and emotions themselves but rather at the expression of moods and emotions. We say Italians are expressive, Canadians are not, Americans are loud, and the Swiss are reserved, while bankers are formal, sports figures are aggressive, and teachers are kind. While this can be useful for us to understand how to interact with those of specific cultural backgrounds, it does not define all the emotions the cultural members possess, but the ones that help preserve the rules of the group.

The author's experience is that all humans have a similar range of possible emotions. That is to say that the *story of injustice* that provokes an emotion that in English we call *anger* exists for all people, regardless of their background. What the culture's relationship with *anger* is and whether it is an emotion that is allowable to feel and express is a different question. As with any country, if you spend time in the United States, you may notice that there are emotions that are accepted and favored and those that are denied or considered distasteful or taboo. *Enthusiasm* and *ambition* are two that you will find deeply intertwined with Americans' way of being. Emotions such as *acceptance* (in the interpretation we presented earlier) or *sadness* are not widely considered valuable or useful. As we said earlier in this interpretation of emotions, it is not helpful to think of emotions as "good" or "bad." Emotions are simply the energy that moves us, guides our actions, and co-creates our stories about ourselves and the world around us. So it is neither praise nor criticism of the United States to notice what emotions are more strongly present and practiced, and doing so can help us understand the observers that Americans are collectively. If we do not consider Americans or any other culture from this perspective, we will end up with a more superficial understanding of them. It goes without saying that any subgroup or individual from any culture can have a very different emotional orientation, but there is a collective view that allows insight into the culture and almost certainly plays some part in the identity of the individual.

All of these observations can be brought to bear on any culture, whether it is ethnic, national, regional, organizational, linguistic, or demographic.

Each will have its own unique set of beliefs, values, rules, and standards, but close examination of these will show a link to its unique emotional makeup. Understanding the value that a culture places on emotions in general or on specific emotions is key to understanding why people from that cultural background go about life as they do. If we truly want to understand others, we must go to significant depth in this area.

Competitive Sports

Sports are physical contests with the objective of determining, according to certain rules, who is best of those competing. But to think that sports are only about physical accomplishment is to miss the importance of the emotions that put the body into action. Without *yearning, passion,* and sometimes *arrogance,* there would be no reason to engage. Without *joy, pride,* and sometimes *smugness,* there would be no thrill in winning. The story of the physical underdog winning against a stronger or more physically talented competitor is an archetypical story that goes back as far as the story of David and Goliath. These stories are built on the emotions of *hope* and *admiration.*

Beyond the emotions of the competitors, there are the emotions of the fans, the coaches, the team owners, the sponsors, and all the others who are part of the sports system. Whether fans are "never-die" or "fair-weather," *loyalty* is their emotional driver. Someone who is happy when their team is losing because it gives them a reason to whine is probably driven by *resentment* or *cynicism.* And those celebrating victory do so because of *pride, satisfaction,* or sometimes *revenge.*

Over the past few decades, one can observe an ever-increasing extremity in the development of sports. Sometimes this is found in the rule changes that allow competitors to go faster or take more risks, but it is even more evident in the development of new sports. The expansion of extreme sports has been generated by the emotion of *excitement*. *Excitement* always seeks to replicate and elevate itself. Thus sporting events seek to build a higher level of excitement, and the emotion feeds on itself. Along with the other emotions, our current sports world is built upon this one. It bodes well for the continued development of sports of this kind, because excitement can never be satisfied, so we can expect ever-increasing extremes of faster, higher, longer, deeper, and at least more apparent risk, because without those, there wouldn't be an increase in excitement.

The Arts

Of all human activities, the ones most often acknowledged as having an emotional root are the arts. Imagine a musical concert and consider how it is designed to generate or elicit specific emotions. It could be *admiration* of the virtuosity of a conductor or classical violinist, the *rage* of a heavy metal concert, or the *delight* produced by a jazz singer. When a particular type of music doesn't deliver on its fundamental emotional basis, it will generally be labeled *disappointing*, which is yet another emotion. In addition to the emotions of the audience, there are the emotions of the musician, painter, or dancer. For them, *passion, yearning*, or *pride* may be part of the mix. *Anger, rage*, or *disappointment* could also fuel their productions. It is easy to imagine those were present when Picasso painted *Guernica*, memorializing the German attack on a civilian village during the Spanish Civil War. The emotions that make up a nation's cultural landscape will likely be reflected in its arts, which means that observing its art can be an entry point to understanding what is and isn't important to its citizens.

Learning to show up as my best self emotionally

Emotional learning has literally changed my life personally and professionally. During an intense weeklong conference, I noticed that I was becoming increasingly overwhelmed mentally and emotionally, with the learning not gelling and anxiety mounting. I began wondering what was "wrong" with me. Why was the learning so hard to access? Why was I struggling? During a seemingly random conversation with my coach I shared my experience, and he asked me a question that significantly altered my life. "Have you considered that you may be an introvert?" In U.S. culture, at least from my perspective, that is not exactly a compliment. We are the land of the bold, the energetic, the achievers—not attributes that I associated with introversion. Plus, on various assessments I had always come out as extroverted, so I had some "scientific validation." Turns out, I was woefully mistaken on many fronts.

Dan, in his low-key but incredibly effective way, helped me to see that I indeed had strong introvert tendencies, that my emotional sensitivity was a part of that makeup, and that by not knowing that, I was unintentionally causing myself suffering. During previous workshops I had always taken a daily walk by myself in nature, but at the conference in question I had instead chosen to be with others at all times. Turns out this wasn't my best move. I needed time by myself, to process, to unwind, to not be stimulated by others. The huge gift that Dan gave me was not only dispelling the many mistaken views I held of introversion, but more importantly helping me get clear on what I need to do to take care of myself so I can show up as my best self emotionally. Thanks to Dan, I can now make effective requests for the alone time that I need and I have the opportunity to show up in life engaged, present, and joyful.

—E.C.

History

History can be and often is presented as a series of facts, dates, and names, and as a result can appear lifeless. But history can also be seen as emotional choreography over time. The economic recessions and depressions that preceded the two world wars can be understood emotionally as a time when many countries were in the mood of *despair* or *hopelessness*. The 1960s are often labeled as a decade of *anger* that produced rebelliousness, and the 1980s as a decade of *greed* that led to imbalanced economies. The Christian crusades were driven by emotions such as *piousness* and *revenge* for having "lost" Jerusalem to Islam, while exploration in all its forms was (and is) fueled by *curiosity, wonder, ambition,* and similar emotions.

Empires are built on the emotions of *trust* (that we the conquerors have the ability to rule better than others) or *distrust* in others having power, *ambition* to have more wealth, or *entitlement* that we "deserve to be the rulers." The fuel for conquest comes from specific emotions, which are related to the stories we believe about ourselves and others. Human history has been described as "an unfolding human drama," and we would add that drama is a heightened expression of emotions.

Geography

The relationship between emotions or moods and geography takes many forms. Natural landscapes elicit emotions ranging from *awe* to *serenity*. Although we talk about visiting specific locations for their "rugged beauty" or "spaciousness," these "reasons" are based in the emotions we experience being in those places. Specific places also have or elicit moods. Islands are often thought of as "isolated," which might come from a mood of *peace* and the belief that we won't be disturbed, or *loneliness* because we feel physically cut off from other people or areas. The mood of cities that grew up along rivers is different from those on the ocean. Mountainous regions generate a different mood than rolling plains or a river delta. Again because emotions and moods are what put us in action, understanding the influence of geography on the mood of a place and its people is essential in order to understand their worldview.

Gender

One of the questions the authors are asked most often is whether we believe that women are "more emotional" than men. If the question is meant to ask whether "women have a wider variety of possible emotions than men," we would say no. It may be impossible to know, but based on our observations, we believe both genders have a similar range of emotions. If the question is meant to ask whether "women feel their emotions more than men," our answer is "we don't know." It has been shown that women have a greater natural ability to discern nuance in color than men and, when trained, have a greater competence in activities such as color-matching photographs. Not all women, but many, have this higher native ability and it is gender related. So women may feel emotions more than men in general, but we would say that to a great degree it depends on what you have learned about emotions growing up and also how much attention and *trust* you put in the sensation of emotions. If the question is meant to ask, "Are women more expressive of their emotions than men?" we would say that is generally true, but feel in a large part this is learned rather than inborn.

The question of "which gender is better at emotions" is, for us, largely academic. Just as anyone with hearing can learn to focus it and to listen differently and in greater detail, or anyone who can walk can learn to walk more efficiently, so it is for emotions. We have all been gifted with emotions as a human attribute, and the work we all face is to learn more about them, practice them, and teach their meaning and navigation to others.

Isms

Nationalism, consumerism, evangelism, socialism, expansionism, imperialism, reductionism, humanism, materialism—these isms (and many more) describe a certainty of belief that is related to several key emotions. When we reach a level of belief that something is not just useful in directing our lives but is the only "true" way to understanding, we have reached the level of an "ism." The underlying emotion of any ism is *righteousness*. This is the emotion that allows us to be unequivocal in our beliefs and absolutely sure our beliefs are "the Truth." Put like that, it may sound like a negative, but actually it allows possibilities that no other emotion does. In order to unreservedly promote or defend an idea, we may need the emotion of *righteousness*. It does cast a large shadow, in that its strength requires that any other belief be seen as wrong, which means they are often disregarded or destroyed.

Climate Change

In the current conversation about global climate change, we look to science (a product of rationalism) to save us. We certainly have the ability to change fundamental aspects of the planet through technology (which is a product of science), but we don't usually consider the emotions that have driven science and technology in the first place. We are *frantic* and increasingly *desperate* for actions that can slow or stop the momentum. There are calls for using less resources, but if we realize that all actions are generated from particular emotions, we can see that this does not address the problem at its most fundamental level. That level is the emotions and moods we humans live in. The emotion of *dissatisfaction* with what we have and a continual striving for development is one driver. The emotion of *entitlement*—that the world owes us something—is another. *Ambition* to build and change is yet another.

Strangely, in all the conversations about coping with climate change or other worldwide issues, scarcely a word is said about the fundamental emotions and moods driving us. It is as if we, collectively, are blind to the power of emotions to move us into action. If it is true that climate change is the result of *human activities*, as is often said, then why have we not adopted emotions that allow us to be *constructively inactive*? What would change if we collectively chose a different set of emotional drivers for our activities? What about *gratitude, wonder, respect*? Would *complacency* or *contentment* be such bad alternatives to *greed* and *achievement*?

But, of course, for this to happen we would need to understand the emotional domain differently. We would need to believe that it is a legitimate domain of learning and that we have the ability to choose the mood in which we live. We would need to see that emotions have as much constructive power as reason and that, in fact, the two are a *wondrous* pairing when used together. We would need to learn to listen underneath the stories we tell ourselves, to the emotion generating the story and the observer those emotions belong to. In short, we would need to shift our understanding of what it is to be human and embrace all of us rather than simply our intellectual gifts.

From guilt to satisfaction

I have always felt guilty about not spending enough time with my children when I'm at work and not spending enough time at work when I'm with my children. My coach helped me distinguish between the emotion of guilt and the emotion of dissatisfaction. This was very liberating to me. I had spent years paralyzed, believing I was feeling guilty, but if the emotion I was feeling was dissatisfaction, then there were a lot of practical things I could do to generate satisfaction. I began asking myself questions like, "What would satisfaction look like?" "What practical steps could I take to achieve it?" "If I did achieve satisfaction, what might that feel like?" Once I began imagining the emotion of satisfaction, our conversation led to a broader issue for me of reflecting this satisfaction in becoming more "queenly" (content, approving, sufficient) in my life. I am still in the middle of this exploration, but I have been enjoying the time with my children and at work more, and am on the long road to becoming more regal in other areas of my life.

—H.W.

Chapter 9

CONCLUSION

Not a moment passes that we are not experiencing an emotion. Nothing we do (or don't do) happens without the energy of emotions. Just as our heart beats without interruption whether we are aware of it or not, so emotions flow through each of us. And just as we often take our hearts for granted, we often don't realize the fundamental importance of our emotions.

We wrote this book with the idea that it might help you become aware, notice, pay attention to, and learn about something that is part of you and a constant companion. Emotions can be one of our most important "assets" or tools and one that enriches every part of life when we develop an understanding and appreciation of them. The stories we have learned that emotions are not useful, in the way, capricious, arbitrary, or something to be ashamed of no longer serve us. It is time to look again and accept a gift that has been waiting for us.

Lucy and I wish you an amazing journey into emotional awareness and literacy. If yours in anything like ours, it will have its moments of wonder and also of terror. You may begin to mark your progress through all the emotions you experience and befriend even when that is uncomfortable. As you journey in this "land of emotions," you will begin to understand things about yourself that you never understood before. Other people will begin to make more sense. In many ways the world will become simpler.

Eventually you will have the opportunity to share what you have learned with others. When that happens, a new understanding of emotions will spread, as has literacy. One day, we believe, emotional literacy will become "common sense" in the way that reading and writing have for the vast majority of human beings. And the world will be a place where things are possible that never were before. That is our dream.

What I learned from envy

Many years ago in a coaching conversation I identified feeling envy about what I believed were opportunities available to someone I knew but not to me. Since I viewed envy as a "bad" emotion, I believed I "shouldn't" feel it and hesitated even saying it out loud. Dan helped me to deconstruct envy, and I was able to understand it differently and to move away from self-pity. I learned that envy meant "I want something in my life that the other person has in theirs." I learned that I could either take it away from them or make a plan to pursue that thing for myself. The emotion I felt had nothing to do with taking it away from them, but only that I had a desire for my life that was unfulfilled. From there I began identifying action steps to get what I wanted. Understanding what envy was trying to tell me and how it was trying to guide me made all the difference.

—S.S.

I can now take the temperature of my emotions

I think the big insight to me was to welcome emotions, to first just become aware of emotions, that they were there, that they were present, that there was a gift in them, and not to fight them. I think I was someone who lived a very compartmentalized life for many, many years, and I think it reflects a certain disconnection from emotions when we live in compartments. I lacked awareness of my emotions except when things got so bad.

For many years I didn't have a subtle awareness of emotions. For me they were like the seasons, but even in the seasons there is a fluctuation in temperature. Today it is more an awareness of temperature than just of the season. Late 2015 was blistering winter for me, and I embraced it. I didn't fight it. My relationship now with emotions is something like my relationship with temperature. I think, "Let's see where I am," and I take the temperature of my emotions. I get curious.

I think this awareness came out of a deep, deep dissatisfaction that the way I was living my life was not working. What I got out of my training was the realization that I wasn't flying blind. I was receiving information from my emotions, but I needed to slow down and listen to them, and from there I could draw conclusions and take action based on what I heard. I felt such relief to know that life was so generous and there was so much guidance there just for me and I only needed to slow down, take it in, listen, pay attention, and become a different observer. Not just of what was happening on the outside but what was happening on the inside.

Life is so different now. It is like night and day. In this huge breakdown I had in late 2014 where I was defrauded and I lost huge sums of money, I felt a lot of sadness. Shame showed up as well, and my emotional learning taught me to just look at what was there. This awareness helped me see that I was bigger than whatever emotion was showing up. I didn't need to be swallowed or swept away by my emotions. When that happened to me, I did not descend into shame, like a vicious cycle where you go down and down and down. I was able to be with what was there because I know now that in life nothing stays. I don't care how crappy you feel, it will change. I don't care how happy you are, it will change. Life never stays the same. I don't think I am anything special; I just think I learned to let my emotions be what they are and to let life be life.

—K.F.

Chapter 10

DICTIONARY OF EMOTIONS AND MOODS

This section is designed to serve as a dictionary for moments you encounter emotions you are unfamiliar with or are unclear about. We have listed each emotion or mood alphabetically by name and include etymology, the information or story it is providing, physical inclination or predisposition, how it is supporting us, and emotions and moods that are related in some way. This is a working list, because as we stated in the beginning, there is not a universal list of emotions and moods, and we are continually enhancing it.

The Unopened Gift

Emotion	Root	Story
Acceptance	Late 14c. "To take what is offered," from Old French *accepter* (14c.) or directly from Latin *acceptare* "take or receive willingly."	"I acknowledge that life is as it is even though I may not agree, endorse, or like it."
Admiration	From Latin *admirari* "to wonder at." From *ad-* "at" + *mirari* "to wonder," from *mirus* "wonderful."	"If I ever do what you do, I want to do it the way you do it."
Adoration	From Latin *adorare* "speak to formally, beseech, ask in prayer," in Late Latin "to worship," from *ad-* "to" + *orare* "speak formally, pray."	"To me, this person or entity is divine."
Adventurousness	From Latin *adventura* "(a thing) about to happen," from *adventurus*, "to come to, reach, arrive at," from *ad-* "to" + *venire* "to come."	"Something amazing will happen in this pursuit."
Affection	From Old French *afection* (12c.) "Emotion, inclination, disposition; love, attraction, enthusiasm," from Latin *affectionem* "a relation, disposition; a temporary state; a frame, constitution."	"I want to show that I like or love this person."
Affront	From Late Latin *affrontare* "to strike against," from Latin *ad frontem* "to the face," from *ad* + *frons*.	"I am being assaulted."

Predisposition	Human Concern	Associated Emotions
To be in stillness without energy in any direction	The ability to align with the facts of life around us, to rest in serenity and peace	Because acceptance appears to be inactive, it can be confused with resignation, which appears similar. The difference is in the story.
To emulate or copy	Identify role models for behavior	Sometimes confused with envy, jealousy, or adoration
To treat with utmost respect or to worship	To bring divinity into human relationships	Related to love but includes admiration rather than acceptance, whereas liking has to do with the enjoyment of being with
To engage fully in exploration	To explore without fear	Similar to enthusiasm but without a divine connection and more for the sensuous joy
To behave in ways that demonstrate liking, loving, or adoring another	To allow the demonstration of loving, liking or admiring	Similar to liking, but a deeper demonstration than simply enjoying being with the other
To recoil	To pull back from situations where we believe we have been assaulted	Similar to indignance, although may precede it. Might result in anger also

Emotion	Root	Story
Aggravation	From Latin *aggravatus*, past participle of *aggravare* "to render more troublesome," literally "to make heavy."	"This situation is irritating and is sapping my energy."
Aggrieved	From Latin *aggravare* "make heavier."	"I feel as if I'm made of lead."
Agony	From Late Latin *agonia*, from Greek *agonia* "a (mental) struggle for victory," originally "a struggle for victory in the games."	"This is unbearable."
Amazement	C.1300, "delusion, bewilderment" (also as a verb, "stupefy, daze"), possibly from Old English *mæs*.	"This is beyond my previous experience and I don't know what to believe."
Ambition	From Latin *ambitionem* "a going around," especially to solicit votes.	"I believe life has possibilities for me and I'm going to go get them."
Amusement	From Middle French *amuser* "divert, cause to muse," from *a* "at, to" + *muser* "ponder, stare fixedly."	"This is enjoyable and diverts my attention."

Predisposition	Human Concern	Associated Emotions
To slow down and shift into a mood of irritation. To complain	To see what keeps us from being in a state of flow	Like irritation, but heavier. Related to frustration, but with less of a moral story
To move very slowly, searching for relief from the sensation of gravity	To slow down and pay attention to serious life changes	Related to sadness as the stage that comes after the realization of something lost
To suffer a pain or struggle	To struggle in spite of enormous pain	Similar to anguish, but more in the physical realm
To be entranced	Shows us that we understand only a part of the universe	Awe, wonder, incredulity
To engage with the world	To engage us with the world and moving into new possibilities	Can be confused with impatience, excitement, or enthusiasm
To engage, consider, ponder	Brings lightness and a sense of play	Could be confused with trivializing. Related to play

Emotion	Root	Story
Anger	Latin *angere* "to throttle, torment," and c.1200, "to irritate, annoy, provoke," from Old Norse.	"I assess an injustice; someone or something is to blame and should be punished."
Anguish	From Latin *angustia* "tightness, straightness, narrowness;" figuratively "distress, difficulty," from *ang(u)ere* "to throttle, torment."	"I feel strangled and bound by this news."
Annoyance	From Late Latin *inodiare* "make loathsome," from Latin *(esse) in odio* "(it is to me) hateful."	"This is deeply distasteful to me."
Anticipation	From Latin *anticipatus*, past participle of *anticipare* "take (care of) ahead of time," literally "taking into possession beforehand," from *ante* "before" + *capere* "to take."	"I'm looking forward to this."
Antipathy	From Latin *antipathia*, from Greek *antipatheia*, "opposed in feeling, having opposite feeling; in return for suffering; felt mutually," from *anti-* "against"+ root of *pathos* "feeling."	"I'm experiencing the opposite emotion than this person."
Anxiety	1620s, from Latin *anxius* "solicitous, uneasy, troubled in mind," from *angere*, *anguere* "choke, squeeze," figuratively "torment, cause distress."	"I believe the future holds danger, but it is unclear what the danger is or where it may come from."

Predisposition	Human Concern	Associated Emotions
To punish the perceived source of the injustice	To create and maintain justice in the world	Often confused with indignance due to similar energy and feelings in the body.
To struggle for understanding	To recognize the collapse of the world as I knew it	Similar to agony but more from a new awareness than physical discomfort
To avoid participation in	To recognize when something is distasteful to me	Somewhat like irritability, but more like disgust than simply irritation
To look forward to participating in or experiencing something	To enjoy the future before it arrives	Related to hopefulness but with more sureness. Similar energy to anxiety but with the belief that the coming event will be enjoyable rather than dangerous
To disagree	To recognize our own emotions relative to another	Opposed to sympathetic and sometimes confused with dislike or contempt
To worry	Alerting us to possible future danger	Similar to fear but not focused on an identified source. Sometimes confused with doubt or collapsed with anticipation

Emotion	Root	Story
Apathetic	From Greek *apatheia* "freedom from suffering, impassability, want of sensation," from *apathes* "without feeling, without suffering or having suffered," from *a-* "without" + *pathos* "emotion, feeling, suffering."	"I don't care."
Apologetic	From Greek *apologia* "a speech in defense," from *apologeisthai* "to speak in one's defense," from *apologos* "an account, story," from *apo-* "from, off" + *logos* "speech."	"I believe something I did caused you pain, although it was not my intention."
Appreciation	1650s, "to esteem or value highly," from Late Latin *appretiatus* "to set a price to."	"This person, place, or thing makes my life better."
Apprehension	From Latin *apprehendere* "to take hold of, grasp," from *ad-* "to" + *prehendere* "to seize."	"Oh, I get it."
Arrogance	C.1300, from Old French arrogance (12c.), from Latin *arrogantia* "assuming, overbearing, insolent."	"I assess others as less intelligent or capable than I am, and therefore I'm better than they are."
Aspiration	From Latin *aspirare* "to breathe upon, blow upon, to breathe."	"I am drawn to climb, grow, or seek something higher."

Predisposition	Human Concern	Associated Emotions
To give up responsibility or participation	To not spend emotional energy	Similar to dispassion, but with a touch of hopelessness.
To acknowledge my part in our breakdown	Allows us to open the possibility of rebuilding trust	Traditionally has meant "admitting fault" but ontologically does not mean saying I was wrong. Pairs with forgiveness.
To express appreciation, to thank	Allows those I value to understand their role in improving the quality of my life	Similar to thankfulness and gratitude
To grasp an idea or come to an understanding	Allows us to know when we newly understand a thing	Often used synonymously with anxiety, but the thing apprehended can have positive or negative consequences
To treat others as less important or intelligent than me; condescend either in language or behavior	To behave as if we are superior morally to others	Contrasts with humility and often a source of pity toward others.
To stretch toward new possibilities; to try new things previously beyond your reach	To grow	Similar to inspiration, but having to do with one's own growth rather than activating others.

Emotion	Root	Story
Attraction	From Latin *attractionem* "a drawing together."	"This is something or someone I'm drawn to be closer to."
Awe	c.1300, *aue*, "fear, terror, great reverence," earlier *aghe*, c.1200, from a Scandinavian source, such as Old Norse *agi* "fright."	"This is bigger and more powerful than I am and could easily injure me."
Baffled	1540s, "to disgrace," perhaps a Scottish respelling of *bauchle* "to disgrace publicly" (especially a perjured knight), which is probably related to French *bafouer* "to abuse, hoodwink."	"I don't understand something I thought I did or that I should."
Bashful	"Gape with astonishment," from *es* "out" + *ba(y)er* "to be open, gape," from Latin *batare* "to yawn, gape," from root *bat*, possibly imitative of yawning.	"I don't want attention put on me."
Befuddled	1580s, "to get drunk" (intransitive); c. 1600, "to confuse as though with drink" (transitive); of obscure origin, perhaps from Low German *fuddeln* "work in a slovenly manner (as if drunk)."	"I am disoriented by my confusion."

Predisposition	Human Concern	Associated Emotions
To move closer, to show interest, to put attention on	Brings us more deeply into contact with people, places and ideas	Connected with curiosity as well as emotions such as delight.
To approach with trepidation, to revere and honor	To help us keep our human power in perspective with the universe around us	Connected with inspiration and wonder, but includes the element of fear
To seek out order and understanding	To be aware of our confusion or misunderstanding	Similar to confusion, but more related to something we thought we understood and now realize we do not.
To stay aside and be sure the attention is not directed at me	To remain anonymous or hidden	Similar to shyness or timidity, but with a touch of self-consciousness or shame
To stumble around mentally in search of understanding	To allow us to search for understanding in a random manner	Similar to baffled and confused, but without the mental clarity available in those

Emotion	Root	Story
Bemused	"To make utterly confused," from *be-* + *muse*. Late 15c., "to divert the attention, beguile, delude," from Middle French *amuser* "divert, cause to muse," from *a* "at, to" + *muser* "ponder, stare fixedly."	"I find this slightly puzzling."
Betrayed	From Latin *tradere* "hand over," from *trans-* "across" + *dare* "to give."	"This person handed me over to the enemy."
Bewildered	1680s, from *be-* "thoroughly" + archaic *wilder* "lead astray, lure into the wilds."	"I'm completely disoriented and lost."
Bewitched	c. 1200, *biwicchen*, from *be-* + Old English *wiccian* "to enchant, to practice witchcraft."	"I can't seem to stop myself."
Blame	Early 13c., from Old French *blasme* "blame, reproach; condemnation."	"Someone caused this wrong."
Bliss	Old English *blis*, also *bliðs* "bliss, merriment, happiness, grace, favor," from Proto-Germanic *blithsjo* from *blithiz* "gentle, kind" + *-tjo* noun suffix.	"This is profoundly satisfying."
Boldness	Old English *beald* (West Saxon), *bald* (Anglian) "bold, brave, confident, strong."	"I will take the initiative to act even though I am unsure or scared."

Predisposition	Human Concern	Associated Emotions
To seek understanding	To generate clarity	Similar to *puzzled* or *confounded*
To be despondent with shock	To recognize when loyalty has been broken	Similar to disloyalty, but betrayal has to do specifically with promises in our relationship
To wander searching for a point of orientation	Allows us to recognize when we are in a territory we do not recognize	Similar to confused, although that is a stage of learning and bewildered is not
Act as if under a spell	Allows us to be irresponsible	Similar to enchanted, but connected with a dark source
Hold accountable the person I believe responsible	Allows us to hold ourselves or others accountable for their actions	Often a part of or found together with anger or resentment
To want to follow the source of the sensation	Shows us the sources of our fulfillment	A kind of active joy that doesn't require external celebration
Initiating action in the face of uncertainty	Allows us to move forward even though feeling doubtful or challenged	Similar to courage, but proactive. Like bravery, but used to overcome doubt rather than fear

Emotion	Root	Story
Boredom	Old English *borian* "to bore through, perforate."	"There is nothing of value to me in this situation."
Bravado	1580s, from French *bravade* "bragging, boasting," from Italian *bravata* "bragging, boasting" (16c.), from *bravare* "brag, boast, be defiant," from *bravo*. The English word was influenced in form by Spanish words ending in -*ado*.	"I will act as though I have more courage than I do."
Bravery	Late 15c. from Middle French *brave*, "splendid, valiant," from Italian *bravo* "brave, bold," originally "wild, savage," possibly from Medieval Latin *bravus* "cutthroat, villain," from Latin *pravus* "crooked, depraved."	"I am acting even though I feel fear."
Calm	From Late Latin *cauma* "heat of the midday sun" (in Italy, a time when everything rests and is still), from Greek *kauma* "heat" (especially of the sun).	"I don't feel energy pulling me in any direction."
Captivated	From Latin *captivus* "caught, taken prisoner," from *captus*, past participle of *capere* "to take, hold, seize."	"I can't get away."

Predisposition	Human Concern	Associated Emotions
To disengage	Points to what we find value in and what we don't	Opposed to curiosity or engagement
To attack or bluff	Allows us to take initiative even when fearful or not inclined to	Can be confused with courage or foolhardiness
To take action that appears risky to oneself or others	To be able to act even when it may put your safety at risk	Related to courage, but closer to boldness.
Stillness	Rest	Serene, peaceful
To remain held	To recognize what a loss of freedom feels like	Similar to enchanted or bewitched, but in a more physical manner

Emotion	Root	Story
Care	Old English *carian, cearian* "be anxious, grieve; to feel concern or interest."	"This is worth attending to."
Caution	From Latin *cavere* "to be on one's guard."	"To remain safe I need to proceed carefully."
Celebration	From Latin *celebratus* "much-frequented; kept solemn; famous," past participle of *celebrare* "assemble to honor," also "to publish; sing praises of; practice often," originally "to frequent in great numbers," from *celeber*.	"I want to show that I believe life is good."
Certainty	From Vulgar Latin *certanus*, from Latin *certus* "sure, fixed, settled, determined."	"I know."
Cheerfulness	From Late Latin *cara* "face"	"This makes me feel good."
Cherish	From Latin *carus* "dear, costly, beloved."	"This is beloved to me."
Commitment	From Latin *committere* "to unite, connect, combine; to bring together," from *com-* "together" + *mittere* "to put, send."	"This initiative deserves my full attention and effort, and I choose to give it freely."

Predisposition	Human Concern	Associated Emotions
Attend to others	Allows us to use our energy to support others. Shows us who and what we are connected to in life	There is a distinction between "caring for" and "caring about." I can care about an unlimited number of things but can only care for what I have energy and time for.
To move in small measured steps	To keep us safe in the presence of possible danger	Prudence
To acknowledge the goodness of an occasion or person	To acknowledge through action what we believe is exceptionally good in life	Like joy but active, as in "jump for joy"
To remain steadfast and not change	To take a stand	Similar to righteousness but not moral by nature as it is
To smile, to laugh	Tells us when we believe good things are happening	Similar to celebration, but less demonstrative
To care for, to protect, to nurture	To hold another closely in spirit	Similar to adoration, but without a divine reference
To act in alignment with our promises	To act in ways consistent with our promises to accomplish in life what we care about	Can be confused with compliance

Emotion	Root	Story
Compassion	From Late Latin *compassionem* from *com-* "together" + *pati* "to suffer."	"Being with this person in their pain is of value."
Compliance	From Latin *complere* "to fill up."	"I will go along with this initiative because I do not believe I have the freedom to decline."
Confidence	From Latin *confidentia*, from *confidentem* "firmly trusting, bold," present participle of *confidere* "to have full trust or reliance," from *com-*, + *fidere* "to trust."	"I believe that it will get done or will happen."
Confoundedness	From Latin *confundere* "to confuse," literally "to pour together, mix, mingle," from *com-* "together" + *fundere* "to pour."	"Everything is mixed up together and I can't make sense of it."
Confusion	From Latin *confusionem* "a mingling, mixing, blending, disorder," noun of action from *confundere* "to pour together."	"I do not see a pattern familiar to me in this situation."
Consternation	From Latin *consternationem* "confusion, dismay," from *consternat-*, "overcome, confuse, dismay, perplex, terrify, alarm."	"Something doesn't seem right."

Predisposition	Human Concern	Associated Emotions
To be with another in their pain	Allows us to be connected with and understand others' emotions without assuming them as our own	Similar to and often not distinguished from pity, empathy, or sympathy
To act because we feel we must	Allows us to act in concert with others even when we do not agree with their directives	Sometimes not distinguished from commitment, but not freely given
To coordinate action without worry	Helps us interact with the world, others, or ourselves	Trust
To question or seek clarity	Helps us know when we are lacking the necessary structure for understanding	Similar to confusion. Can lead to fear, frustration, or curiosity as next steps.
To attempt to "figure it out" or to integrate an idea into our understanding	Is a predictable step in learning until we create an order that includes the new ideas	Similar to curiosity, but can include the assessment that "something is wrong." Related to confounding and consternation
To go slowly in determining if the path is safe	Stops our actions to consider the prudence of them	Related to prudence, but with more fear or anxiety

Emotion	Root	Story
Contempt	Latin from past participle of *contemnere* "to scorn, despise," from *com-*, intensive prefix + **temnere* "to slight, scorn."	"Nothing good can come from you, and I assess myself superior to you."
Contentment	From Latin *contentus* "contained, satisfied."	"I do not need to change anything."
Courage	From Latin *cor* "heart."	"I will take action even though I am scared."
Covetous	From Latin *cupiditas* "passionate desire, eagerness, ambition."	"I want it to be mine no matter the consequences."
Curiosity	From Latin *curiositatem* "desire of knowledge, inquisitiveness."	"There is something interesting or of benefit to me here."
Cynicism	In reference to the ancient philosophy, from Greek *kynikos* "a follower of Antisthenes," literally "doglike," from *kyon* (genitive *kynos*) "dog." Supposedly from the sneering sarcasm of the philosophers, but more likely from *Kynosarge* "Gray Dog," name of the gymnasium outside ancient Athens (for the use of those who were not pure Athenians) where the founder, Antisthenes, a pupil of Socrates, taught.	"I distrust others' apparent good intentions."

Predisposition	Human Concern	Associated Emotions
To treat others in a condescending manner	To know our standard relative to respecting others	Related to disrespect. Similar to scorn
To be comfortable with things as they are	To be at rest	Similar to satisfaction
To act in the presence of fear	Allows us to act in the presence of fear	Precursor to boldness
To want to take what is not mine	To know what we are passionate about owning or claiming	Envy, greed, and jealousy
To ask questions	To gain understanding of our experiences in order to learn	Opposed to boredom
To reject all positive or hopeful possibilities	To challenge ungrounded excitement	Can be seen as active resignation

Emotion	Root	Story
Dejection	From Latin *deiectus* "a throwing down, felling, fall, to cast down, destroy; drive out; kill, slay, defeat," from *de-* "down" + *-icere*, comb. form of *iacere* "to throw."	"I can't believe this has happened to me and don't like it at all."
Delight	From Latin *delectare* "to allure, delight, charm, please," frequentative of *delicere* "entice."	"This is wondrous and enjoyable."
Denial	From Latin *denegare* "to deny, reject, refuse" from *de-* "away" + *negare* "refuse, say no."	"I am unwilling to consider the possibility."
Depression	Early 14c. "put down by force," from Old French *depresser*, from Late Latin *depressare*, frequentative of Latin *deprimere* "press down," from *de-* "down" + *premere* "to press."	"The situation has robbed me of hope and energy."
Desire	Latin *desiderare* "long for, wish for; demand, expect," original sense perhaps "await what the stars will bring," from the phrase *de sidere* "from the stars."	"I want to be in connection with this thing or person."
Despair	From Latin *desperare* "to despair, to lose all hope," from *de-* "without" + *sperare* "to hope."	"I have no hope, see no possibilities."
Despise	From Latin *despicere* "look down on, scorn," from *de-* "down" + *spicere* "look at."	"This is beneath my status."

Predisposition	Human Concern	Associated Emotions
To deny and resist what has occurred	Shows the importance of the thing we were expecting to happen	Similar to disappointment. Related to incredulity, but with a darker mood.
To be in the experience	To tell us what we enjoy and what pleases us	Related to happiness, joy, and fun
To ignore the experience	Allows us to function in moments when the truth would immobilize us	To remain naïve by choice
To remain idle	To stop and consider where I might find hope and energy	Related to disappointment, but more severe. Similar to hopelessness or despondence
To seek what I long for	To know what things, people, and experiences we want in our lives	Similar to yearning
To withdraw and give up trying	To reach "the bottom," to experience the lowest	Related to despondence but less severe. Can be confused with being in a state of depression
To condescend either in words or action, scorn	To see how we evaluate our position relative to others	Can be confused with hate, but tends to be about the person rather than an injustice

Emotion	Root	Story
Despondence	From Latin *despondere* "to give up, lose, lose heart, resign, to promise in marriage" (especially in phrase *animam despondere*, literally "give up one's soul")	"I have lost everything."
Devastation	From Latin *devastare* "lay waste completely," from *de-* "completely" + *vastare* "lay waste," from *vastus* "empty, desolate."	"This experience empties me of all my desire to take action."
Dignity	From Latin *dignitatem* "worthiness," from *dignus* "worth, worthy, proper, fitting."	"I am worthy."
Disappointment	From Middle French *desappointer* (14c.) "undo the appointment, remove from office," from *des-* + *appointer* "appoint."	"I expected things to happen differently."
Disgust (synonymous with distaste)	Latin from *des-* "opposite of" + *gustare* "to taste"	"This experience leaves a bad taste in my mouth."
Dislike	From Latin *dis-* "apart, in a different direction, between" + Middle English shortening of Old English *gelic* "like, similar," from Proto-Germanic **galika-* "having the same form," literally "with a corresponding body"	"This experience is not enjoyable."
Dismay	From Latin *de-* + **exmagare* "divest of power or ability"	"I do not have the power I thought I had."

Predisposition	Human Concern	Associated Emotions
Immobility	Helps us see what is important to us at the most fundamental level—of the soul	Similar to despair, but more severe or deeper
To withdraw and grieve	To understand what things in life we believe are unthinkable	Can be confused with depression or despair
To honor myself, to generate self-respect	Allows us to set and protect our personal boundaries	Can be confused with arrogance or narcissism
To try to maintain our story of how life "should" be	Informs us that our idea of how life will go and how life is going are not aligned	Similar to dismay, but more pronounced
To reject, turn away, or not participate	Keeps us from engaging in things that don't align with our values	Similar to revulsion, but not as strong. Sometimes confused with scorn or hate when about people.
To avoid spending time with	Tells us what we enjoy in life and what we don't	Can be confused with righteousness
To withdraw from the effort of choosing	Helps us recognize the limits of our powers	Similar to disappointment but not as intense

Emotion	Root	Story
Dispassion	Directly from Latin *dis-* "apart, in a different direction, between," from Late Latin use of *passio* to render Greek *pathos*, literally "suffering," from *polian* "to endure."	"I can see the passion but am not caught by it."
Dissatisfaction	Directly from Latin *dis-* "apart, in a different direction, between," *satisfacere* "discharge fully, comply with, make amends," literally "do enough," from *satis* "enough" + *facere* "perform."	"I assess I do not have enough of x in my life."
Distaste (synonymous with disgust)	From Vulgar Latin **tastare*, apparently an alteration (perhaps by influence of *gustare*) of *taxtare*, "evaluate, handle"	"This experience literally leaves a bad taste in my mouth."
Distraction	From Latin *distractus*, "draw in different directions."	"I cannot keep my attention on one thing."
Dividedness	From Latin *dividere* "to force apart, cleave, distribute," from *dis-* "apart" + *-videre* "to separate."	"My emotions are pulled in opposing directions."
Doubt	Rooted in the Latin *dubiosus* (English *dubious*), which meant "vacillating, fluctuating, or wavering."	"I am unsure."
Dread	Late 12c. a shortening of Old English *adrædan*, contraction of *ondrædan* "counsel or advise against."	"I could lose everything, and cannot cope with the possibility."

Predisposition	Human Concern	Associated Emotions
To stand aside literally and figuratively, to not be involved emotionally	Allows us to observe emotions and cares from an outside perspective	The emotion being referred to when we talk about being "objective"
To find ways of having more x	To know what I want more of in life	Sometimes seen as negative, but can be understood simply as information about my desires or needs
To reject, turn away, or not participate	Keeps us from engaging in things that don't align with our values	Similar to revulsion, but not as strong. Sometimes confused with scorn or hate when about people.
Lack focus on one thing	Tells us where it is most important for us to put our attention	Can be confused with compliance or ambivalence
To vacillate	To show us what we care about even when the choices are in opposition	Similar to ambivalence, but with attachment to both possibilities
To hesitate or to move ahead with prudence	To alert us that we are in a new territory; calls us to pay attention to our preparation	Confused with anxiety or fear. Not related to danger, but rather to new situations
To give up or, at most, proceed with deep caution	Puts us on alert to what may destroy or seriously damage us	Strong in the way fear can be, but vague like anxiety

Emotion	Root	Story
Ease	C.1200, "physical comfort, undisturbed state of the body; tranquility, peace of mind," from Old French *aise* "comfort, pleasure, well-being; opportunity," which is of unknown origin, despite attempts to link it to various Latin verbs; perhaps Celtic.	"This is taking very little effort in my estimation."
Ebullience	1590s, "boiling," from Latin *ebullientem* "to boil over," literally or figuratively, from *ex-* "out" + *bullire* "to bubble."	"I am so excited I cannot regulate or contain it."
Ecstasy	"Mystically absorbed," from Greek *ekstatikos* "unstable, inclined to depart from."	"I am in the presence of the incomprehensible."
Effervescence	From Latin *effervescentem*, "to boil up, boil over," from *ex-* "out" + *fervescere* "begin to boil," from *fervere* "be hot, boil."	"This is so exciting I can't contain myself."
Elation	From Latin *elationem*, "a carrying out, a lifting up." Late 14c. "inordinate self-esteem, arrogance," especially "self-satisfaction over one's accomplishments or qualities, vainglory," from Old French.	"I can hardly believe my good fortune."

Predisposition	Human Concern	Associated Emotions
To do what we are doing with joy and appreciation	Tells us what activities we have competence in and accomplish with little effort	Related to happiness or delight, but more related to energy than enjoyment
To engage with tremendous energy and enthusiasm	Tells us what things we care about and cannot restrain ourselves from acting upon	Similarities to excitement, elation, effervescence, and enthusiasm
To be absorbed	Helps us see the enormity and incomprehensibility of the universe	Intense passion or eroticism. Can be similar to awe but without the element of fear
To boil over with energy and excitement	To make us aware of our intense excitement	Similar to excitement, but beyond. Related to elation, but without the self-conscious aspect
To enjoy, share, and celebrate	Allows us to celebrate good fortune or accomplishments	Similar to excitement, but specifically about my sense of good fortune and/or accomplishment

Emotion	Root	Story
Embarrassment	1670s, "perplex, throw into doubt," from French *embarrasser* (16c.), literally "to block," from Italian *imbarrazzo*, from *imbarrare* "to bar," from assimilated form of *in-* "into, upon" + Vulgar Latin **barra* "bar"	"I have done something I do not want others to know about."
Empathy	A translation of Greek *empatheia* "passion, state of emotion," from assimilated form of *en* "in" + *pathos* "feeling."	"I am feeling what the other is feeling."
Enchantment	Late 14c. literal and figurative, from Old French *enchanter* "bewitch, charm, cast a spell" (12c.), from Latin *incantare* "to enchant, fix a spell upon."	"I feel like I'm under a spell."
Enjoyment	From stem of Old French *enjoir* "to give joy, rejoice, take delight in," from *en-* "make" + *joir* "enjoy," from Latin *gaudere* "rejoice."	"I like doing this."
Ennui	From French *ennui*, from Old French *enui* "annoyance."	"I find this annoying."
Enthusiasm	From Greek *enthousiasmos* "divine inspiration," from *enthousiazein* "be inspired or possessed by a god, be rapt, be in ecstasy," from *entheos* "divinely inspired, possessed by a god," from *en* "in" + *theos* "god."	"The cause I am committed to is noble or even divine."

Predisposition	Human Concern	Associated Emotions
Desire to hide what we have done from others	Helps us know how we believe it's best to behave in relation to others	Related to guilt and shame, but not as intense, and more about actions than being
To be in resonance with the emotions of the other	Helps us to understand the emotions others are experiencing	Similar to sympathy, but a stronger connection with subject. Often confused with compassion.
To be in wonder	To feel the powers around us that we can't see and don't understand	Similar to bewitched, but without a shadow, lighter
To continue to willingly participate	To experience the pleasant side of life	Delight
To move away from or end the experience	To know what we don't like or don't enjoy in life	Similar to annoyance, irritability
To act on behalf of a cause greater than myself or ourselves.	To allow us to connect with cares and causes bigger than ourselves	Often confused with excitement, but has a connection with "the gods" or the divine which excitement does not

Emotion	Root	Story
Entitlement	From Late Latin *intitulare* "give a title or name to," from *in-* "in" + *titulus* "title."	"I deserve to have it because the world owes it to me."
Envy	From Latin *invidia* "envy, jealousy" from *invidus* "envious, having hatred or ill-will," from *invidere* "to envy, hate," earlier "look at (with malice), cast an evil eye upon," from *in-* "upon"+ *videre* "to see."	"I deserve it more than he/she does, and if I cannot have it, I want him/her to lose it."
Equanimity	From Latin *aequanimitatem* "evenness of mind, calmness; goodwill, kindness," from *aequanimis* "mild, kind," literally "even-minded," from *aequus* "even, level" + *animus* "mind, spirit."	"Considering all sides fairly will give the best result."
Eroticism	From Greek *erotikos* "caused by passionate love, referring to love," from *eros* "sexual love."	"I desire to become one with another."
Euphoria	Medical Latin, from Greek *euphoria* "power of enduring easily," from *euphoros*, literally "bearing well," from *eu* "well" + *pherein* "to carry."	"I am having an experience of extraordinary well-being."
Excitement	From Latin *excitare* "rouse, call out, summon forth, produce," frequentative of *exciere* "call forth, instigate," from *ex-* "out" + *ciere* "set in motion, call."	"This energizes me and I want to continue it."

Predisposition	Human Concern	Associated Emotions
To take whatever I see that I want and to whine if I cannot have it	To see what we believe has been promised us that we have not received	Is in opposition to gratitude
To undermine the person or persons who possess or have achieved what I believe is rightfully mine	To know what we would like to have or be in life	Often not distinguished from jealousy, but is provoked by covetousness, while jealousy is prompted by fear
To consider in a calm and even-minded manner	Allows us to consider life from a calm center and to treat all parties with the same respect	Allows us something close to being "objective" while acknowledging we are always in an emotion
To meld with the other	Allows us to unite fully with another	Often not distinguished from passion, sexuality, or lust
To remain in the experience	Helps us understand the degree to which well-being can be profoundly pleasurable	Can be confused with ecstasy, excitement, or eroticism
To do more; to experience it again; literally *to set in motion from the outside*	To know what in life gives us energy	Can be confused with joy, delight, or enthusiasm

Emotion	Root	Story
Exhaustion	From Latin *exhaustus*, past participle of *exhaurire* "draw off, take away, use up, empty," from *ex-* "off" + *haurire* "to draw up" (as water).	"I can't go on."
Exhilarated	From Latin *ex-* "thoroughly" + *hilarare* "make cheerful."	"I am extremely happy with this situation."
Expectant	From Latin *expectare* "await, look out for; desire, hope, long for, anticipate; look for with anticipation," from *ex-* "thoroughly" + *spectare* "to look."	"I am waiting and am keenly aware I am waiting."
Exuberant	From Latin *exuberantem* "overabundance," present participle of *exuberare* "be abundant, grow luxuriously," from *ex-* "thoroughly" + *uberare* "be fruitful."	"Life is full of promise."
Faith	From Latin *fides* "trust, faith, confidence, reliance, credence, belief," from root of *fidere* "to trust."	"I believe even though I have no evidence."
Fascination	From Latin *fascinatus*, "bewitch, enchant, fascinate," from *fascinus* "a charm, enchantment, spell, witchcraft," which is of uncertain origin.	"There is something here I am very attracted to, even though I don't understand why."
Fear	From Old English *fær* "calamity, sudden danger, peril, sudden attack."	"Something specific in the future is likely to harm me."

Predisposition	Human Concern	Associated Emotions
To stop	To know when we have reached our limit of energy	Can be confused somatically with resignation or acceptance
To enjoy with a heightened level of energy	Allows us to celebrate and appreciate life's experiences	Often confused with excited. Joyful but with more energy.
To be aware there is something we want to occur in the near future	Helps us understand what we desire to occur for us or to us	Similar to anxious, but without the concern
To throw myself into life's possibilities	To understand how abundant life can be	Similar to enthusiasm, although not associated with divinity but more with life on the human plane
To act from our beliefs	To act without the need of evidence or in the face of evidence to the contrary	Like trust, it allows us to act but does not require assessing sincerity, competence, or reliability
To pursue and seek connection with	To draw us into things and people even when we don't understand why	Similar to enchantment or bewitched
To run away	To know specifically what we believe may harm us	Related to anxiety, worry, anguish, dread

Emotion	Root	Story
Foolish	From Vulgar Latin use of *follis* in a sense of "windbag, empty-headed person."	"Thinking through this is unnecessary."
Forgiveness	Old English *forgiefan* "give, grant, allow; remit (a debt), pardon (an offense)," also "give up"; from *for-* "completely," + *giefan* "give."	"Something you did caused me pain, but I will not use it against you in the future."
Frustration	From Latin *frustrationem*, "a deception, a disappointment."	"It should have happened already."
Fury	From Latin *furia* "violent passion, rage, madness," from or related to *furere* "to rage, be mad."	"To attack as a madman."
Garrulousness	From Latin *garrulus* "talkative, chattering."	"Arguing is fun."
Generosity	From Latin *generosus* "of noble birth," figuratively "magnanimous, generous," from *genus* "race, stock."	"I desire to give to others so they can share my good fortune."
Gracious	From Latin *gratia* "favor, esteem, regard; pleasing quality, good will, gratitude"	"It is right to treat this person with kindness."
Gratitude	From Latin *gratia* "favor, esteem, regard; pleasing quality, good will."	"Life is a gift."

Predisposition	Human Concern	Associated Emotions
To act without consideration of the consequences	To act without thinking	Somewhat like naiveté, but more related to stupidity than ignorance
To coordinate action with the knowledge that I may be hurt again	To declare the past closed when we have future interactions	Pairs with apology
To strike out against the person or thing I believe is keeping "it" from happening	To know when we have reached our limit of effort and need a change	Often not distinguished from irritation or aggravation, but has a different message
Attacking with all my energy	To attack without reservation	Similar to rage, but more about attacking than destroying
To argue for entertainment	To take positions simply for the enjoyment of the controversy	Sometimes seen as orneriness or irritability, but is done intentionally
To give	To be able to give without attached conditions or expectations	Related to kindness, but is about giving rather than including
To treat well, to honor	To allow us to treat others with kindness and honor	Kindness, magnanimity
To be a gift	To see all of life as a gift	Often not distinguished from thankfulness, which has to do with trading

Emotion	Root	Story
Gravity	From Latin *gravis* "weighty, serious, heavy, grievous, oppressive."	"This is very serious."
Greed	Old English *grædig* (West Saxon), *gredig* (Anglian) "voracious, hungry," also "covetous, eager to obtain."	"I want it."
Grief	From Latin *gravare* "make heavy" from *gravis* "weighty."	"I feel I will never recover."
Grimness	Old English *grimm* "fierce, cruel, savage, dire, painful," from Proto-Germanic **grimmaz*.	"This is bad or is going to be bad."
Guilt	Old English *gylt* "crime, sin, fault, fine," of unknown origin.	"I have broken my own standards."
Happiness	Late 14c., "lucky, favored by fortune, prosperous"; of events, "turning out well," from *hap*, "chance, fortune" + *-y*	"I am content with life as it is."
Hate	From PIE root **kad-* "sorrow"	"The world would be better off without this person or thing."
Helplessness	Old English meaning "unable to act for oneself," c. 1200, from *help* (n.) + *less*	"I am incapable of doing it myself."

Predisposition	Human Concern	Associated Emotions
To act without humor or levity	To know what we believe is serious and profound	Seriousness. Opposed to delight.
To take without consideration or regard for others or for our needs	To take	Confused with covetousness, but not necessarily about a specific person; more general
To search for a meaning in the event that produced the gravity	To find meaning in and recover from grave situations	Related to sadness, but the stage that comes after the realization of something lost
To move into a situation with deep caution	To be aware of a difficult situation	Similar to despair, but not as profound; seriousness
To punish myself	To know my own values and when I have betrayed them	Often confused with shame, but takes care of private rather than public identity
To enjoy the present moment	To know what I believe is good or pleasant in life	Similar to joy and satisfaction
To remove from our world in whatever ways possible	To identify those things or people we do not want to share the world with	A strong dislike
To wait for the help of others	To allow us to receive when we are incapacitated	Despair, but not necessarily negative; resignation, but due to true incapacity

Emotion	Root	Story
Hilarity	From Latin *hilaritatem* "cheerfulness, gaiety, merriment."	"This is beyond funny."
Honor	From Latin *honorem* "dignity, office, reputation," of unknown origin.	"This is how tradition says things should be done."
Hope	Old English *hopian* "wish, expect, look forward (to something)," of unknown origin.	"The future will be better than the present, and I want to be there."
Hopelessness	Old English *hopian* "wish, expect, look forward (to something)," of unknown origin + "lacking, cannot be, does not," from Old English *-leas*	"There are no possibilities in this situation."
Horror	From Latin *horror*, literally "a shaking, trembling, shudder, chill," from *horrere* "to bristle with fear, shudder."	"I can't imagine a worse fate."
Hubris	From Greek *hybris* "wanton violence, insolence, outrage," originally "presumption toward the gods."	"My opinion is as if from the gods. I can do no wrong."
Humiliation	From Latin "to be humbled"	"This experience reminded me that I have limits."

Predisposition	Human Concern	Associated Emotions
To laugh uncontrollably	To break the seriousness of life	Enjoying the silliness of something without belittling it
To act according to traditional standards and expectations	To maintain the order of the past	Sometimes not distinguished from respect, but is about past tradition rather than acknowledging the quality of a thing or person
To move toward the future	To allow us to see what we believe a possible future could be	Contrasts with nostalgia, which is about the past, while hope is about the future
To give up and not act	To recognize that nothing we do will make a difference and to surrender	Resignation, but a more grounded awareness that I do not have the power needed to change things
To tremble and freeze mentally	To be aware of the worst possible fate	Similar to intense, mind-numbing fear
To act with extreme arrogance	To act beyond our humanness, and when we see others react, reminds us of our humanness	Similar to arrogance but stronger. Opposed to humility
To consider my limits	To align ourselves to the reality of our capabilities and power	Similar to humility, but includes a touch of shame

Emotion	Root	Story
Humility	From Latin *humilis* "lowly, humble," literally "on the ground," from *humus* "earth." "To lower (someone) in dignity."	"I am human and have the limits of a human."
Immodesty	From Latin *in-* "not, opposite of" + *modestus* "keeping due measure."	"I will behave in a way more provocative than expected."
Impatience	Directly from Latin *in-* "not," + *patientia* "endurance, submission," also "indulgence, leniency; humility; submissiveness; submission to lust"; literally "quality of suffering."	"I don't understand why this hasn't happened yet."
Incredulousness	From Latin *incredulus* "unbelieving, incredulous," from *in-* "not" + *credulous* "worthy to be believed."	"I cannot believe it."
Indifference	From Latin *indifferentem*, "not differing, not particular, of no consequence, neither good nor evil," from *in-* "not, opposite of" + *differens*, present participle of *differre* "set apart."	"It doesn't make any difference to me."
Indignation	Latin from *indignus* "unworthy," from *in-* "not, opposite of" + *dignus* "worthy."	"I refuse to be treated in this way because it violates my standards."

Predisposition	Human Concern	Associated Emotions
To act without the pretense that I am either more or less than I am	To align ourselves to the reality of our capabilities and power	Opposed to hubris. Related to humiliation, but without any sense of shame
To act outside of cultural standards	To challenge limiting cultural standards	Similar to imprudence, but in regard to behavior rather than risk
To look for ways to pass by what is blocking us	Makes us aware that there might be a way to move through things more quickly	Similar to irritable, but more rationally aware. Often confused with anger, but has to do with my standards rather than injustice.
To question how something is possible	To challenge the information we are being given	Similar to amazement, but with less capacity to believe the situation
To follow whatever course of action others suggest or take	To surrender to the leadership of others or to let go of situations that are not particularly important to us	Similar to ambivalence, but more a lack of care than the ability to support various positions. Sometimes confused with apathy.
To protect myself and my boundaries	To take care of myself and maintain a sense of self-respect	Often confused with anger, but the predisposition is to protect myself rather than to punish another

The Unopened Gift

Emotion	Root	Story
Infatuation	From Latin *infatuatus*, past participle of *infatuare* "make a fool of," from *in-* "in" + *fatuus* "foolish."	"I am completely taken by this person and don't care if I look silly or stupid."
Innocence	Latin *innocentia*, from *innocens* "harmless, blameless."	"I don't know how this happened."
Inspiration	Latin from *in-* "in" + *spirare* "to breathe"	"I can prompt or induce others to action."
Intrigued	From Latin *intricatus* "entangled," past participle of *intricare* "to entangle, perplex, embarrass," from *in-* "in" + *tricae*	"This really, really interests me."
Irascibility	From Latin *irasci* "be angry, be in a rage," from *ira* "anger."	"This provokes me."
Ire	Middle High German *erken* "to disgust."	"This disgusts me."
Irresponsible	From Latin *ir-* + *respons* "to respond." Retains the sense of "obligation" in the Latin root word.	"I can act without regard to my obligations."
Irreverence	Mid-14c., from Latin *irreverentia* "want of reverence."	"I don't need to treat this as if it's the only truth."
Irritability	Latin *irritatus*, past participle of *irritare* "excite, provoke."	"This bothers me."

Predisposition	Human Concern	Associated Emotions
To pursue without self-consciousness	To engage with what I find attractive without gravity	Similar to lust but with lightness, and more about pursuing than melding with
To deny responsibility	To remain untouched or ignorant	Similar to denial, but comes from unawareness or blindness. Native naiveté.
To influence others to act in new ways	To support the growth and exploration of others	Similar to aspiration, but is focused on activating others.
To investigate	To know what is of profound interest to us	Similar to attracted, but more often about an idea or thing than a person
To lash out or to fight	To move to protecting or attacking	Similar to anger, but without the driver of injustice
To push it away or get rid of the source	To "spit out" or throw out what I dislike	Similar to disgust, but from a different linguistic root
To act according to my whims rather than as promised or expected	To allow me to be free to act spontaneously but also to know the line that defines my obligations	Similar to unaccountable, but more conscious
To not take seriously	Allows us to see things without the lens of gravity or untouchability	Confused with disrespect, but is more in the way of ignoring that others hold a thing sacred
To stop or get away from the cause	To understand that I am at my limit emotionally	Similar to aggravation, but less severe

Emotion	Root	Story
Jaded	"Bored by continual indulgence," 1630s.	"I find this ridiculous, trite, and boring."
Jealousy	From Late Latin *zelus* "zeal."	"I am afraid you/he/she will take something I have."
Joy	From Latin *gaudia*. c.1200, "feeling of pleasure and delight;" c.1300, "source of pleasure or happiness," from Old French *joie* (11c.).	"Life is good and I want to celebrate it."
Judgmental	From Latin *iudicare* "to judge, to examine officially; form an opinion upon."	"I know what is morally correct."
Kindness	From Old English *gecynde* "natural, native, innate," originally "with the feeling of relatives for each other."	"I am being treated as one of the family."
Lascivious	From Late Latin *lascivia* "lewdness, playfulness, frolicsomeness, jollity," from *lascivus* "lewd, playful, frolicsome, wanton."	"This is wicked in a sexual way."
Laziness	Probably comes from Low German *laisch* "weak, feeble, tired." Thought to be from *lay* as *tipsy* is from *tip*.	"I have no desire to take action."

Predisposition	Human Concern	Associated Emotions
To dismiss the importance of a thing	To see what interests us and what we are tired of	Similar to disgusted, but comes from familiarity rather than distaste
To try to protect what I have from the other	To see what we fear losing in life	Often not distinguished from envy, which is prompted by covetousness, while jealousy is prompted by fear
To savor the moment, feel pleasure or delight, and to continue living	To feel goodness, pleasure	Related to happiness and satisfaction
To assess others morally as to their goodness or badness as humans or in human action	To set a standard for right behavior in our lives or in our community	Opposed to acceptance as an emotion
To feel welcome	To easily connect and accept the attention of others	Similar to tenderness, but not as much concerned with creating safety
To flirt	To connect sexually	Related to eroticism, but is strongly sexual in nature
Do little or nothing	To rest	Slothful

Emotion	Root	Story
Liking	Middle English shortening of Old English *gelic* "like, similar," from Proto-Germanic **galika-* "having the same form," literally "with a corresponding body."	"I am comfortable with this person or thing and would like to spend more time with it/them."
Livid	From Latin *lividus* "of a bluish color, black and blue."	"What was done is extremely wrong."
Loneliness	c. 1600, "solitary, lone," from *lone + -ly*	"I am without company and therefore not whole."
Lonesomeness	From Old English *all ana* "unaccompanied, all by oneself," from *all* "all, wholly" + *an* "one."	"I am without company, but nonetheless whole."
Love	Old English *lufian* "to cherish, show love to; delight in, approve."	"I accept and cherish this person as he or she is."
Loyalty	Latin *legalem*, from *lex* "law."	"I will protect and support those in my group."
Lust	Old English *lust* "desire, appetite, pleasure; sensuous appetite."	"I want this."

Predisposition	Human Concern	Associated Emotions
To be with	To be at ease and enjoy the company of another person or thing	Joy, tenderness, acceptance
To punish strongly	To be able to raise our energy to take care of what we believe is wrong	Anger, rage
To seek out others for company	Urges us to seek out others to complete our sense of self	Often confused with lonesomeness, but includes the feeling of a void when alone
To enjoy our solitude	To know that we can enjoy life without the company of others	Often confused with loneliness, but does not include feeling a void when alone
To legitimize another as they are	To maintain a connection regardless of circumstances	Often confused with liking, which is enjoying being with another rather than profound acceptance of the other
To defend the group of which I am part	To take care of the integrity of the group	Sometimes confused with commitment or accountability, but is about taking care of a group identity and not our promises
To engage without consideration of consequences	To know what we desire	Related to passion, but more from the perspective of using the other rather than melding with

Emotion	Root	Story
Magnanimous	From Latin *magnanimus* "high-minded," literally "great-souled"	"I want to use my resources to take care of others."
Maudlin	From *Magdalene* (Old French *Madelaine*), woman's name, originally surname of Mary the repentant sinner forgiven by Jesus in Luke 7:37. In paintings, she often was shown weeping as a sign of repentance.	"I have done wrong; I know it and am seeking forgiveness."
Melancholy	Late Latin *melancholia*, from Greek *melankholia* "sadness," literally (excess of) "black bile," from *melas*, "black" + *khole* "bile." Medieval physiology attributed depression to excess of "black bile," a secretion of the spleen and one of the body's four "humors."	"I am sad and not inclined to action."
Mischievous	From Old French *meschief* "misfortune, harm, trouble; annoyance, vexation," verbal noun from *meschever* "come or bring to grief, be unfortunate" (opposite of *achieve*), from *mes-* "badly" + *chever* "happen, come to a head," from Vulgar Latin *capare* "head."	"This will probably provoke others, and that is why I want to do it."
Misery	From Latin *miseria* "wretchedness."	"The world is a terrible place."

Predisposition	Human Concern	Associated Emotions
To use our resources to take care of others	To use our resources to take care of others	Similar to generosity, but is not as much about giving as taking care of
To weep	Allows us to pause to recognize and take responsibility for the wrongs we have done	Related to guilt and often an emotion or state that follows guilt. Can also be related to shame in the same way.
To wallow in our lack of energy or motivation	To know when we are physically out of balance	Sadness, indifference, laziness
To intentionally provoke others for our own amusement	To test others' limits or to play at provoking others	Playful
To suffer	To help us see the worst aspects of human life	Related to agony, anguish, grimness

Emotion	Root	Story
Modesty	From Latin *modestus* "keeping due measure."	"I am behaving in a proper way."
Morose	"Gloomy," from Latin *morosus* "morose, peevish, hypercritical, fastidious," from *mos* "habit, custom."	"Everything is wrong, and that is the cause of my mood."
Mortification	From Late Latin *mortificare* "cause death, kill, put to death," literally "make dead."	"I am deeply embarrassed and feel that dying (at least figuratively) would be the best solution."
Naïveté	From Latin *nativus* "not artificial," also "native, rustic," literally "born, innate, natural."	"Everything in life should be good and the way I want it to be."
Nostalgia	1770, "severe homesickness considered as a disease," Modern Latin, coined 1668 in a dissertation on the topic at the University of Basel by scholar Johannes Hofer. From Greek *algos* "pain, grief, distress"+ *nostos* "homecoming," from PIE *nes-* "to return safely home."	"Life was better in the past and I would like to return there."
Obligation	From Latin *obligare* "to bind, bind up, bandage."	"I have no choice but to do this."

Predisposition	Human Concern	Associated Emotions
To act in accordance with custom or tradition	To demonstrate we are part of a group through our considered action and thereby remain a part of it	Similar to prudence, but concerned with social behavior rather than risk
To wallow in the story of how bad life is	To help us see what life would look like if indeed everything was wrong	Misery, grimness
To hide	To help us see the importance of our personal identity	Embarrassment, shame, guilt
To ignore what appears unpleasant or ugly	To help us see the need to take responsibility for our knowledge and actions	Related to denial, innocence and lack of acceptance
To reminisce and orient my thinking toward the past	To know that life can be good and to see the possibility it will be so again	Can be contrasted with regret, which is looking to the past and wishing it had been lived differently
To act whether I want to or not	To take action even when it is not what we would freely choose	Related to responsibility, accountability, compliance, and commitment

Emotion	Root	Story
Obsequiousness	From Latin *obsequiosus* "compliant, obedient," from *obsequi* "to accommodate oneself to the will of another," from *ob* "after" + *sequi* "to follow."	"My thoughts, ideas, and actions are not as important as others'."
Offensive	From Latin *offendere* "to hit, strike against," figuratively "to stumble, commit a fault, displease, trespass against, provoke."	"I'd like to say something to hurt this person."
Optimism	From Latin *optimus*, "the best."	"I know good things and bad things happen in life, but mostly good things happen to me."
Orneriness	1816, American English dialectal contraction of *ordinary*. "Commonplace," hence "of poor quality, coarse, ugly." By c.1860 the sense had evolved to "mean, cantankerous."	"I am contrary to every possibility."
Panic	From Greek *panikon*, literally "pertaining to *Pan*," the god of woods and fields, who was the source of mysterious sounds that caused contagious, groundless fear in herds and crowds, or in people in lonely spots.	"We are doomed if we don't get away."

Predisposition	Human Concern	Associated Emotions
To follow the lead of others, to be subservient due to lack of self-trust	To see the need to take a stand for ourselves in life	Can be confused with humility or service. Similar to compliance, but lacking more in the area of self-trust or self-respect.
To speak in a way that injures the other	To see the power of words	Related to anger, but not connected with injustice
To act freely in situations where I don't know what the outcome will be	To live in a way that keeps me looking for the good things coming my way	Contrasts with pessimism
To respond harshly to every interaction	Allows us to separate ourselves from others	Irritable, but without the need of provocation
To run	To flee danger	Fear, terror

Emotion	Root	Story
Paranoia	From Greek *paranoia* "mental derangement, madness," from *paranoos* "mentally ill, insane," from *para-* "beside, beyond" + *noos* "mind."	"Everyone wants to harm me."
Passion	From Late Latin *passionem*, "suffering, enduring."	"I have a deep desire to be close to another."
Peace	From Latin *pacem*, "compact, agreement, treaty of peace, tranquility, absence of war."	"All is well."
Pensiveness	Late 14c., from Old French *pensif* "thoughtful, distracted, musing" (11c.), from *penser* "to think," from Latin *pensare* "weigh, consider."	"The solution will probably come through reflection."
Perplexity	From Latin *perplexus* "involved, confused, intricate." The Latin compound would be *per* "through" + *plexus* "entangled, to twine, braid, fold"	"My thoughts are all tangled up and intertwined."
Perseverance	From Latin *perseverantia* "steadfastness, constancy."	"I will continue trying no matter what."
Pessimism	Latin *pessimus* "worst," originally "bottommost."	"I know good things and bad things happen in life, but mostly bad things happen to me."

Predisposition	Human Concern	Associated Emotions
To fear and avoid others	To remove ourselves from perceived danger from others, especially when they are not behaving as if to hurt us	Fear, anxiety
To be as close to another as humanly possible	To produce closeness	Often confused with eroticism or sexuality
To move with ease	To rest without worry	Tranquility, serenity
To consider possibilities thoughtfully	To consider possibilities, to examine a variety of options	Similar to prudence, but is related to thinking rather than taking physical action
To try to untangle or straighten our thoughts	To move toward putting our thoughts in a logical or rational order	Confusion, befuddlement, bewilderment
To continue efforts toward a goal	To move forward in spite of obstacles	Similar to boldness in moving forward, but without the presence of fear
To act reluctantly and without enthusiasm	Allows us to live without undue expectations	In contrast to optimism. Similar to hopelessness, but not as deep

Emotion	Root	Story
Petulance	From Latin *petulantem* "wanton, forward, saucy, insolent," present participle of *petere* "to attack, assail; strive after; ask for, beg, beseech."	"This is ridiculous, and I will say so."
Pity	From Latin *pietatem*, "piety, loyalty, duty."	"I see suffering, but feel superior because it is their fault they are suffering."
Playful	Old English *plegan*, "move rapidly, occupy or busy oneself, exercise; frolic; make sport of, mock; perform music."	"This is fun."
Pleased	From Latin *placere* "to be acceptable, be liked, be approved," related to *placare* "to soothe, quiet."	"This is nice or enjoyable."
Pride	Mid-12c. to "congratulate (oneself)"	"I have done a good job and I want to tell others."
Prudence	Directly from Latin *prudentia* "a foreseeing, foresight, sagacity, practical judgment."	"There might be danger, so it is best to move ahead carefully."
Rage	From Medieval Latin *rabia*, from Latin *rabies* "madness, rage, fury."	"Nothing is worth saving."
Rancor	From Latin *rancere* "to stink" and Late Latin, "grudge, bitterness."	"Life is bitter."

Predisposition	Human Concern	Associated Emotions
To ridicule or attack in a dismissive way	To name what I believe is ridiculous or unfounded	Disrespect, but more about an idea or situation than a person
To look down on the sufferer as less than me	To acknowledge that, at times, having superior abilities or knowledge is needed to help others	Often confused with compassion or empathy, but has the quality of superiority to the other
To act for the joy of acting	To enjoy acting	Delight
To enjoy	To experience well-being	Enjoyable, happy, content
To celebrate my accomplishments	To share with others things we believe we have done well	Sometimes not distinguished from arrogance or narcissism
To move ahead cautiously whether in thought or action	To move into action at a pace that allows us to adjust to changing circumstances	Similar to caution. Opposed to impatience.
To destroy without regard	To eliminate the old which we believe is not worth saving	Related to anger, but more associated with perceived evil than injustice. Fury
To hate life; to live as if we've been wronged by life	To taste what life would be like if there was no sweetness	Spite, orneriness

Emotion	Root	Story
Rapacious	From Latin *rapaci-*, stem of *rapax* "grasping," itself from stem of *rapere* "to seize"+ *-ous*.	"It is mine to take."
Rebellious	From Latin *rebellis* "insurgent, rebellious," from *rebellare* "to rebel, revolt," from *re-* "opposite, against," + *bellare* "wage war," from *bellum* "war."	"I am breaking the rules and I know it."
Regret	"To look back with distress or sorrowful longing; to grieve for on remembering," late 14c., from Old French *regreter* "long after, bewail, lament someone's death; ask the help of."	"Life would be better if I had or had not done x."
Remorse	From Latin *remordere* "to vex, disturb," literally "to bite back," from *re-* "back" + *mordere* "to bite."	"I should have acted differently."
Resentment	From Latin *re-* + *sentire* "to feel."	"Life should not be this way; I shouldn't have to do that."
Resignation	From Latin *resignare* "to check off, annul, cancel, give back, give up," from *re-* "opposite" + *signare* "to make an entry in an account book," literally "to mark."	"Nothing I do will make any difference."
Resilient	From Latin *resilientem* "inclined to leap or spring back."	"I can bounce back."

Predisposition	Human Concern	Associated Emotions
To take	To take without regard to the ownership of others	Similar to entitlement, but more active
To violate rules consciously	To break out of social convention	Related to mischievousness and discontent, but more active and serious
To punish myself for doing or not having done something in the past	To reflect on choices we made and use them as guides in future ones	Often indicates a lack of boldness in the past. Like nostalgia, but looking at what was lost rather than what was enjoyable
To blame myself for actions in my past	To know which past behaviors were out of alignment with our values and their costs	Related to guilt, but doesn't include self-punishment. See regret.
To resist with the secret intention of getting even	To know what we believe to be unfair	Opposed to acceptance. Sometimes confused with anger.
To not take action, inaction	To remove ourselves from interaction	Can be confused with acceptance, but closer to hopelessness
Return to center	To re-center ourselves after being pushed off balance	Always begins with acceptance of what is

Emotion	Root	Story
Resolve	From Latin *resolutus*, "untie, unfasten, loose, loosen." The notion is of "breaking (something) into parts" as the way to arrive at the truth of it and thus make the final determination.	"This requires action."
Respect	From Latin *respectus* "regard, a looking at," literally "act of looking back (or often) at one," from *re-* "back" + *specere* "look at."	"This thing or person is deserving of being treated as important."
Responsibility	From Latin *respondere* "respond, answer to, promise in return."	"It is something I must do."
Restlessness	An inability to "repose, cease from action," Old English *ræstan*, *restan* "take repose by lying down; lie in death or in the grave; cease from motion, work, or performance; be without motion; be undisturbed, be free from what disquiets."	"I can't stop moving."
Reverence	From Latin *reverentia* "awe, respect," from *revereri* "to stand in awe of, respect, honor, fear, be afraid of."	"This is worthy of my respect and honor."

Predisposition	Human Concern	Associated Emotions
To act	To move into action	Sometimes confused with ambition or enthusiasm. More grounded than ambition and not necessarily connected with a bigger cause as with enthusiasm
To treat well, to consider and listen to	To know which things or people we hold as legitimate and valuable	Similar to dignity, but generally about how we treat ourselves or others rather than boundaries
To take ownership of (usually a situation)	To declare my leadership	Related to accountable, but more proactive
To move or seek movement, whether it is effective or not	Gives us the energy to continue seeking new possible actions	Similar to irritable, but without a negative connotation. Opposed to peaceful, serene, calm
To treat with utmost respect and even fear	To treat the other as legitimate and deserving of respect and honor	Related to awe, but without the element of fear

Emotion	Root	Story
Revulsion	From Latin *revulsionem*, "a tearing off, act of pulling away," noun of action from past participle stem of *revellere* "to pull away," from *re-* "away" + *vellere* "to tear, pull."	"This disgusts me."
Righteousness	Early 16c. alteration of *rightwise*, from Old English *rihtwis*, from *riht* + *wis* "wise, way, manner."	"My beliefs are the only correct beliefs."
Rigor	From Latin *rigorem*, "numbness, stiffness, hardness, firmness; roughness, rudeness."	"Always doing this in this way will produce the best results."
Sacrifice	From Latin *sacrificus* "performing priestly functions or sacrifices," from *sacra* "sacred rites." Sense of "act of giving up one thing for another."	"I do for others in ways that deplete me."
Sadness	From Old English *sæd* "sated, full, having had one's fill (of food, drink, fighting, etc.), weary of."	"I have lost something I cared about."
Safety	From Latin *salvus* "uninjured, in good health, safe," related to *salus* "good health," *saluber* "healthful."	"I won't be injured."

Predisposition	Human Concern	Associated Emotions
To turn away from	To know what we want to get away from	Related to disgust, but stronger, or dislike and distaste, but much stronger
To dismiss others' point of view and beliefs and to demand obedience	To be sure of our beliefs	Can be confused with confidence, but more absolute and with arrogance
To choose and maintain a specific form	To repeat as closely as possible in order to produce consistent results	Sometimes confused with persistence, which is continued trying, while rigor is maintaining form
To care for others while disregarding my needs	To give up ourselves for the sake of others	Is sometimes confused with service, but depletes us, whereas service nurtures us
To withdraw and grieve	To know what we care about in life	Often confused with depression, melancholy or maudlin
To be at ease	To rest and move freely	Similar to peace or serenity, but most often about avoiding injury

Emotion	Root	Story
Satisfaction	Latin *satisfacere* "discharge fully, comply with, make amends," literally "do enough," from *satis* "enough." From PIE root *sa- "to satisfy" + *facere* "perform."	"I have enough."
Savoring	From Latin *saporem*, "taste, flavor," related to *sapere* "to have a flavor."	"This is a delicious experience."
Scarcity	From Vulgar Latin *scarsus*, "pluck out."	"There is not enough."
Scared	1590s, alteration of Middle English *skerren* (c.1200), from Old Norse *skirra* "to frighten; to shrink from, shun; to prevent, avert," related to *skjarr* "timid, shy, afraid of," of unknown origin.	"Something is likely to happen that will injure me."
Scorn	"To break off (someone's) horns," from Vulgar Latin *excornare* (source of Italian *scornare* "treat with contempt"), from Latin *ex-* "without" + *cornu* "horn."	"This person or thing is not worthy of my respect."
Sedate	From Latin *sedatus* "composed, moderate, quiet, tranquil," past participle of *sedare* "to settle, calm," causative of *sedere* "to sit."	"I'm fine, okay, not disturbed."

Predisposition	Human Concern	Associated Emotions
To appreciate, savor, or enjoy	To allow us to know what is enough or when we are sufficiently full	Often contrasts with entitlement, which focuses on what I believe I deserve rather than what would be enough
To embrace the experience and enjoy it	Allows us to relish and enjoy life	Similar to enjoyment, but deeper and more visceral
To try to get more	To be sure we will have enough for the future	A type of fear especially related to not having enough resources
To run away	To avoid perceived danger	Fear, but not as specific. Closer to anxiety, but from Northern European rather than Latin linguistic root
To ridicule or belittle	To know our standard relative to respecting others	Similar to contempt, but more active
To be still	To allow us to be still even when we are not clear that all is well in life	Similar to tranquil, but not as freely relaxed

Emotion	Root	Story
Self-recrimination	From Medieval Latin *recriminatus*, past participle of *recriminari* "to make charges against," from Latin *re-* "back, again"+ *criminari* "to accuse."	"I shouldn't have done x."
Sensual	Directly from Late Latin *sensualis* "endowed with feeling." Meaning "connected with gratification of the senses."	"I like the sensations or feelings this produces."
Sensuous	1640s, "pertaining to the senses" apparently coined by Milton to recover the original meaning of *sensual* and avoid the lascivious connotation that the older word had acquired.	"I am having this experience through my senses."
Sentimental	From Medieval Latin *sentimentum* "feeling, affection, opinion," from Latin *sentire* "to feel."	"This recalls tender emotions from another time."
Serenity	From Latin *serenus* "peaceful, calm, clear."	"All is well."
Service	Latin *servitium* "slavery, condition of a slave, servitude," also "slaves collectively," from *servus* "slave."	"I do for others in a way that nurtures us both."

Predisposition	Human Concern	Associated Emotions
To punish myself	To punish myself for what I believe I have done wrong. To hold myself accountable	Related to guilt, account-able and responsible, but actively self-punishing
To engage in the activity	To enjoy the sensations of an experience	Can be confused with sensuous or sexual
To be aware while engaging in the activity	To be aware of the sensations of an experience	Can be confused with sensual or sexual
To be tender toward the past	To be able to reflect on what was tender in the past	Similar to nostalgia, but focused on tenderness rather than on what I believe was good
To remain at ease	To rest without concern	Similar to peace, tranquility
To provide for others in a manner that does not deplete me	To know what for me is acting in a caring manner toward others	Often used interchangeably with sacrifice, but ontologically service means our efforts nurture us, while sacrifice depletes us

Emotion	Root	Story
Sexy	1905 from *sex* + *-y*. Originally "engrossed in sex"; sense of "sexually attractive" is 1923, first in reference to Valentino.	"Sex is what is important here."
Shame	The best guess is that this is from PIE **skem-*, from **kem-* "to cover" (covering oneself being a common expression of shame).	"I have broken the standards of my community."
Shyness	Late Old English *sceoh* "timid, easily startled," from Proto-Germanic **skeukh(w)az* "afraid." German *scheuchen* "to scare away."	"I don't want to be seen."
Sincere	From Latin *sincerus*, of things, "whole, clean, pure, uninjured, unmixed," figuratively "sound, genuine, pure, true, candid, truthful."	"I believe what I am saying is true."
Skepticism	Greek *skeptikos* (plural *Skeptikoi* "the Skeptics, followers of Pyrrho"), meaning "inquiring, reflective" (the name taken by the disciples of the Greek philosopher Pyrrho, who lived c.360–c.270 BCE), related to *skeptesthai* "to reflect, look, view."	"I doubt that this is true."
Slothful	Late 12c., "indolence, sluggishness," formed from Middle English *slou, slowe*.	"I have no desire to hurry even if I'm assessed as lazy."

Predisposition	Human Concern	Associated Emotions
To desire or to move toward engaging sexually	To know what attracts us to engage sexually	Related to eroticism, passion. Can be confused with sensuality or tenderness.
To hide from the judgment and punishment of my community	To recognize what the standards of the community are and when we have transgressed them	Often not distinguished from guilt
To hide	To stay distant from situations we are unsure of	Similar to timidity, but from different linguistic roots
To be transparent	A basis for assessing trust and thus coordination of action	Similar to honesty
To hesitate, dismiss, or seek further information	To help us ensure that we are understanding something new correctly	Like cynicism, but less severe and with more possibility for change. Similar to incredulity, but tries to reject what is rather than simply disbelieving it. Mild cynicism.
To move slowly and deliberately without energy	To move slowly	Laziness

Emotion	Root	Story
Smugness	Possibly an alteration of Low German *smuk* "trim, neat," from Middle Low German *smücken* "to adorn" (originally "to dress," secondary sense of words meaning "to creep or slip into").	"I know better than you."
Sorrow	From Old English *sorg* "grief, regret, trouble, care, pain, anxiety."	"I feel pain that this happened."
Stubborn	Late 14c., of uncertain origin. Earliest form is *stiborn*.	"I'm not changing my belief."
Stupendousness	Late Latin *stupendus* "to be wondered at," connected to Latin *stupere* "be stunned, be struck senseless, be aghast, astounded, or amazed."	"This is wonderful."
Surprise	From *sur-* "over" + *prendre* "to take," from Latin *prendere*, contracted from *prehendere* "to grasp, seize."	"I didn't think this would happen."
Surrender	From Old French *surrendre* "give up, deliver over" (13c.), from *sur-* "over"+ *rendre* "give back."	"I give up."
Suspicion	From Latin *suspiciosus, suspitiosus* "exciting suspicion, causing mistrust."	"I am not sure I trust this person or situation."

Predisposition	Human Concern	Associated Emotions
To condescend	To recognize when we feel superior or to know when others are feeling superior	Similar to arrogance, but less overt. Sometimes confused with pride.
To wish it had not happened	To know what we care about and hope to happen differently in the future	Similar to sadness, but not necessarily about something we've lost
To refuse to change, especially in regard to beliefs	To take a stand for what we believe is correct	Similar to perseverance, but more about maintaining where I stand than moving forward
To be immobilized	To recognize a wonderful and amazing occurrence	Similar to incredulous, but more related to wonder than disbelief
To struggle with a sudden change	To help us know when something has changed suddenly	Often precedes disappointment or resilience. Mild incredulity.
To allow control to go to the other	To stop fighting or resisting	Similar to resignation, but is done willingly
To question another's motives or story	Allows us to remain safe even when we are being told there is nothing to be concerned with	Can be confused with skepticism, cynicism, or distrust

Emotion	Root	Story
Sympathy	Directly from Late Latin *sympathia* "community of feeling, sympathy," from Greek *sympatheia* "fellow-feeling, community of feeling," from *sympathes* "having a fellow feeling, affected by like feelings," from assimilated form of *syn-* "together"+ *pathos* "feeling."	"My emotions are similar to another's emotions, and through that I understand them."
Tenderness	From Latin *tenerem*, "soft, delicate; of tender age, youthful."	"I am safe in this relationship."
Terror	From Latin *terrorem* "great fear, dread, alarm, panic; object of fear, cause of alarm; terrible news," from *terrere* "fill with fear, frighten."	"I'm certain something horrible will happen to harm me."
Thankfulness	Old English *pancian, poncian* "to give thanks, to recompense, reward."	"Trading something of value for something in return."
Thrill	Early 14c., "to pierce, penetrate," metathesis of Old English *pyrlian* "to perforate, pierce."	"This experience is exciting and I want more."
Timid	From Latin *timidus* "fearful, afraid, cowardly."	"I will be safer if I don't expose myself."

Predisposition	Human Concern	Associated Emotions
To agree with others as to their situation and its impact or meaning	Allows us to understand how others experience the world emotionally	Often confused with empathy and compassion
To provide safety for others	Allows us to invite others to a safe place close to us	Often confused with eroticism or sexuality; has to do with creating safety through closeness rather than closeness for the sake of sex or melding
To hide by trying to run away	Allows us to identify those things we believe pose immediate threats	Intense fear. Sometimes confused with horror, but more about the fear than the harm I anticipate.
To engage in mutual exchange	Allows us to acknowledge those things that we believe have value	Can be confused with gratitude, but is about trading rather than gifting
To seek out more of the same	To know where the edge of comfortable experience is for us	Excitement, delight
To hide or stay out of the action	Allows us to observe from a distance to gauge danger	Similar to shyness

Emotion	Root	Story
Tiredness	"To weary," also "to become weary," Old English *teorian* "to fail, cease; become weary; make weary, exhaust," of uncertain origin.	"I can't go on."
Tolerant	From Latin *tolerare* "to endure, sustain, support, suffer," literally "to bear."	"I will put up with this person or situation until it changes to my liking."
Triumphant	From Old Latin *triumpus*, probably via Etruscan from Greek *thriambos* "hymn to Dionysus." Late 14c., "success in battle, conquest," also "spiritual victory" and "a procession celebrating victory in war."	"I won" or "We won."
Triviality	From Latin *trivialis* "common, commonplace, vulgar."	"Nothing is worth considering seriously."
Trust	From Old Norse *traust* "help, confidence, protection, support." Old High German *trost* "fidelity," German *Trost* "comfort, consolation," Gothic *trausti* "agreement, alliance."	"I can rely on the person or thing to do as they promise."
Unaccountability	1640s, "inexplicable," meaning "not liable to be called to account."	"I can behave as I like without consequences."

Predisposition	Human Concern	Associated Emotions
To slow down or stop to rest	Allows us to see the limits of our energy	Exhaustion, but not as severe
To put up with another for the moment	Allows us to take a step toward being in relationship	A step toward acceptance, but holds the judgment that the other is misguided or wrong
To celebrate winning publicly	The ability to acknowledge winning or gaining what I/we have gone after	Closely related to pride. Can be confused with smugness or arrogance.
To belittle or diminish the importance of everything	Can allow us to move out of gravity or deny grave situations	Sometimes confused with delight or amusement, but includes element of disrespect
To coordinate action	The ability to interact with the world, others, or with ourselves	Similar to confidence, but from Northern European linguistic root rather than Latin. Sometimes not distinguished from naïveté
To act according to my whims rather than as promised or expected	To be able to act without constraints	Irresponsibility

Emotion	Root	Story
Uncertainty	From Vulgar Latin *certanus*, from Latin *certus* "sure, fixed, settled, determined" + *un*.	"I am not sure I know."
Vanity	From Latin *vanitatem* "emptiness, aimlessness; falsity."	"I feel empty or worthless, but want to avoid it."
Vengeance	From Latin *vindicare*, "vindicate" from *vim dicare* "to show authority," from *vim*, accusative of *vis* "force" + root of *dicere* "to say."	"I will get even."
Wariness	From Old English *wær* "prudent, aware, alert."	"Something here may hurt me if I don't pay attention closely."
Wistfulness	Perhaps from obsolete *wistly* "intently" (c.1500), of uncertain origin. Middle English *wistful* meant "bountiful, well-supplied," from Old English *wist* "provisions."	"I wish for the past that had all that I needed or wanted."
Wonder	Old English *wundor* "marvelous thing, miracle, object of astonishment."	"I don't understand this experience, but I am enjoying it anyway."
Wrath	Old English *wræððu* "anger," from *wrað* "angry."	"It is my place to punish."

Predisposition	Human Concern	Associated Emotions
To remain where we are because we're unsure which of the possible paths is best	To wait for clarity	Similar to ambivalence, but in that case all paths are equal, or indecision, which is caused by the same lack of clarity
To try to appear more beautiful, skilled, or gifted than I am	To help me appear to be more than I am in my relationships with others	Related to arrogance and narcissism in that I am pretending to be more than I am
To act in such a way that I gain control of the other to do as I choose	Allows me to understand at the deepest level what ways of being treated are unacceptable to me	Related to resentment, but with a stronger focus on getting even for perceived injustice
To proceed with close attention and awareness	Helps us to move prudently in unknown areas	Similar to prudence, but with more concern and focus on possible sources of danger
To want to re-create the times that were more abundant	Shows us what from the past we consider good	Similar to nostalgia, but includes a bit more pain and not action-oriented. Like regret, but not as deep.
To remain in the experience	To connect us with elements in the world bigger and more powerful than ourselves	Similar to awe, but without the fear. Curiosity on a cosmological scale.
To punish relentlessly	To allow us to punish enormous injustice	Rage, anger, vengeance

Emotion	Root	Story
Wretchedness	Old English *wrecca* "wretch, stranger, exile," from Proto-Germanic **wrakjon* "pursuer; one pursued."	"I am being relentlessly pursued and driven out."
Xenophobic	1903, from *xeno-* "foreign, strange" + *-phobia* "fear."	"Anyone not like me is dangerous."
Yearning	Old English *giernan* "to strive, be eager, desire, seek for, beg, demand."	"There is nothing in life more important than pursuing this."
Zeal	"Passionate ardor in pursuit of an objective or course of action," late 14c., from Old French.	"I am really, really excited to do this."

Predisposition	Human Concern	Associated Emotions
To cower, to back away, to exile oneself	To show us where we do not belong or are not wanted	Despair, resignation
To exclude any person different from me or us	To preserve the culture as it is	Opposite to love, which is legitimizing the other as different
To pursue the source of the yearning	To tell us what we believe are the most important possibilities in life	Desire, eroticism. Opposed to indifference or ambivalence.
To throw oneself into action	To put us into energetic action	Delight, ambition, enthusiasm

The Unopened Gift

ABOUT THE AUTHORS

Lucy Nuñez and Dan Newby are both coaches, coach trainers, and facilitators. They are married and live in Barcelona. Lucy completed studies in Psychology, Human Relations and Organizational Consulting, Group Dynamics, and several models of coaching. Her professional background includes training coaches at the Escuela Europea de Coaching and a long career as a trainer and consultant in the business field. She is a native of Venezuela and emigrated to Spain in 2001. Dan is a U.S.-born educator, coach, mentor, and writer with 25 years of business leadership experience. For eight years he was a Senior Course leader for Newfield Network Coaching School in the United States, Canada, and Europe, and now works independently. Both are keenly interested in human learning, how it is applied culturally, organizationally and personally and, of course, emotions.

RESOURCES/MORE INFORMATION

Our vision is that this book will grow and morph over time. You are invited to participate in that process by sending the authors your questions, ideas, examples or emotions you believe should be added:

    Lucy Nuñez can be contacted at lucynunez.alg@gmail.com
    Dan Newby can be contacted at dan@dannewby.me

Ongoing updates and event offerings can be found at www.dannewby.me

Our Work

Workshops: We offer workshops several times a year for coaches who would like to deepen their understanding of emotions and how to use emotions as a tool to increase the effectiveness of their coaching. In the United States, we offer two five-day workshops each year in New Mexico. Registration is limited to twelve participants. In Europe the location varies. All workshops are in English with Spanish-language support.

Coaching: Both executive and personal coaching are possibilities. We have experience working with executives and managers at all levels and from many cultural backgrounds. Dan coaches only in English and Lucy in Spanish. Coaching can take place in person or through video conferencing.

Coach Mentoring: We offer mentoring for coaches, whether for certification renewal or to enhance skills. These sessions can be individual or group. They are generally done by video conference, but can be arranged in person.

Facilitation: Both Lucy and Dan have a long history of facilitation for groups, particularly in the area of leadership development. We offer programs customized to the needs of your team or organization.

Online Training: We offer online training in Emotions and Coaching and related themes. These programs are asynchronous and can be accessed through any internet connection. They can be customized or combined with in-person work.

ACKNOWLEDGMENTS

We would like to thank the hundreds of students, coachees, coaches, teachers, friends, family and facilitators who have supported us and that we have had the pleasure of working with on our respective journeys. Each has contributed in their own way to our learning and in turn to this book.

In particular, we thank Julio Olalla and Rafael Echeveria, who were instrumental in pioneering this interpretation of emotions and who we regard as unique and gifted teachers.

Thank you to Bethany Kelly of Publishing Partner for her direction and support, and to our manuscript reviewers Kim Ebinger, Clement Graham, Reiner Lomb, Will Newby, Mirko Kobiela, Curtis Watkins, and Nancy Graham, who provided invaluable feedback.

A special note of appreciation for Douglas Harper, the creator of www. etymonline.com. In this book and in all of our work we find his site to be a tremendously valuable source of learning and clarification on the origins of our English words, and we encourage you to support his efforts.

INDEX

Index

Index

Index

CPSIA information can be obtained
at www.ICGtesting.com
Printed in the USA
BVHW041936090521
606895BV00014B/695

9 780692 855782